The Urbanization of Modern America
A Brief History

THE HARBRACE HISTORY OF THE UNITED STATES

The Urbanization
of Modern America
A Brief History

Zane L. Miller
University of Cincinnati

Under the General Editorship of
John Morton Blum, Yale University

 HARCOURT BRACE JOVANOVICH, INC.
New York   Chicago   San Francisco   Atlanta

Frontispiece: Bruce Davidson/Magnum Photos, Inc.

The author wishes to thank the Wadsworth Publishing Company for granting permission to use
portions of his essay "The Black Experience in the
Modern City," in Raymond Mohl and James
Richardson, eds., *The Urban Experience,*
scheduled for publication during April 1973; and
the *Journal of American History* for permitting
him to reproduce here in slightly altered and
augmented form his article, "Boss Cox's
Cincinnati: A Study in Urbanization and Politics,
1880–1914," which appeared in the March
1968 issue.

ISBN: 0-15-593656-5

Library of Congress Catalog Card Number:
72-92361

Printed in the United States of America
*Page 231 constitutes a continuation of the
copyright page.*

Preface

The urban historian seeks to do two things. His first concern is to discover how cities have grown. This "internal" view concentrates on describing and analyzing the changing shape and physical size of cities, their population and economic composition, the location of segments of the population and of commercial and industrial facilities, the nature of urban politics and government, and the interrelationships among all these factors. His second task is to assess the role of cities in the overall history of the nation. This "inside out" perspective focuses on the way in which cities influence broad political developments, such as the Revolution or the New Deal, or how they affect economic events, such as the Industrial Revolution or the coming of twentieth-century corporate society. The first task requires close attention to particular places in particular times, while the second requires a broader view with less emphasis on events in one city.

The mode of analysis most appropriate for constructing a synthesis of both the "internal" and "inside out" approach to urban history might be called ecological. By treating the urban environment as a complex of interdependent factors, ecologic analysis permits the student to examine the manner in which both city dwellers and the socioeconomic and political systems we call cities influenced and accommodated to shifts in their surroundings. This mode of analysis also assumes that decisions made by individuals and by communities as they confront change are based in part on their perception of the past.

There are several other reasons for attempting a general view of American urban history. First, it provides a way to establish order out of a history that at first glance seems utterly chaotic. American cities at any point in time look astonishingly diverse. They possess varying population and economic structures, they differ in age and in regional settings, and they exhibit differential rates of growth. Yet by taking a general view and concentrating on common patterns of internal growth and on the relationship between cities and the larger society it is possible to formalize American urban history into four periods. While not ignoring spatial, or geographic, considerations, one can speak, in this view, of the preindustrial city of the seventeenth, eighteenth, and early nineteenth centuries; of the industrializing city of the mid-nineteenth century; of the industrial city of the late nineteenth and early twentieth centuries; and of the postindustrial city of the mid- and late twentieth century.

Yet another reason for such a treatment of our urban past is that it may offer material on which to base constructive responses to the contemporary metropolitan crisis. In recent years growing numbers of Americans have become convinced that this generation faces a set of urban problems unique in both its variety and intractability. This notion derives in part from the general failure to recognize that congestion, crime, violence, pollution, poverty, and class and ethnic tensions have been prominent features of America's urban scene almost from its beginning in the seventeenth century. Indeed, the American city has been almost continually in crisis, and an analysis of the elements of these crises that illuminates the way in which they acquired their current configuration ought to prove useful both in deciding which are most important and in unraveling the connections among them.

Equally important, a broader understanding of urban history should help mitigate the contemporary metropolitan crisis by providing an alternative to what has been called the pathology approach to the study of city life.

This book, more than most of its genre, is a cooperative enterprise. I have cited those works on which I relied most heavily, but some people played a larger or more direct role. Richard C. Wade's influence on my knowledge of and thinking about urban history has been deep and continuing, so much so that I can scarcely tell where his contributions end and mine begin. My colleagues and students at the University of Cincinnati, especially those who participated in our interdisciplinary urban research seminar over the past three years, have helped me broaden my perspective and sharpen my arguments, and Tony Deye aided in the process of working out the initial organization of the volume. Jill Patrick patiently deciphered and typed early stages of the manuscript, and Kris Ruggiero made helpful stylistic and substantive suggestions while typing a later version. Michael Frisch of the State University of New York at Buffalo provided a penetrating analysis that was indispensable in correcting deficiencies in the original text. Stephan Thernstrom of the University of California at Los Angeles also read the manuscript at various stages in its production and gave me helpful commentaries. I am also indebted to the National Endowment for the Humanities and the University of Chicago Center for Urban Studies for postdoctoral fellowships which gave me the time and resources to study the black urban experience. Most important, Janet Miller encouraged me to undertake the task and provided valuable critiques, steady support, and quiet understanding. None of these people bears any responsibility for the book's shortcomings but all helped make the job easier, stimulating, and instructive.

ZANE L. MILLER

For Janet

Contents

xi

part one

DEVELOPMENT

The City 1

The first era in American urban history stretches from the early seventeenth century to about 1840. Throughout these years the total urban population remained small and the cities restricted in physical area. At the first federal census in 1790 city dwellers comprised merely 5.1 percent of the total population, and only two places numbered more than 25,000 inhabitants. Fifty years later only 10.8 percent of the nation's population fell into the urban category, and only one city, New York, contained more than 250,000 people.

Largely because of the unsophisticated modes of transportation, even the more populous places in the early nineteenth century remained compact enough that an individual could easily walk from one end to the other.

THE CITY AS AN ORGANIZING FORCE

Though diminutive by modern standards, these "walking cities" performed a variety of functions. One was economic. Throughout the premodern era this aspect of urban life remained so overwhelmingly commercial that virtually every city owed its vitality to trade. Yet urbanites concerned themselves not only with facilitating access to and stimulating extractive-agricultural pursuits in their rural and undeveloped hinterlands; they also collected and processed goods from these areas, and distributed that produce to other cities in return for merchandise funneled back into local urban and hinterland markets. From the beginning, then, and increasingly in the eighteenth and early nineteenth centuries, cities served as centers of both commerce and simple manufacturing.

The early cities also had important noneconomic functions. Since libraries, museums, schools, colleges, printers, and newspapers needed a substantial clientele and supporting services, cities and the larger early towns, with their concentrations of population, tended to serve as centers of educational activities and as points from which information radiated into the countryside. In addition, the towns, with people of diverse occupational, ethnic, racial, and religious affiliations, became focuses of formal and informal associations devoted to fostering the security and enhancing the well-being and influence of each group. These various groups, including those devoted to politics, often sought to advance their particular interests by undertaking projects that incidentally benefited other groups in the city and influenced the larger society as well. For example, competing religious denominations established colleges in the cities that trained clergy, who went out on both urban and rural assignments, and attracted students who patronized shops adjacent to the colleges. Other groups operated within a similar competitive-cooperative system. As a result, growing towns organized and dominated their surrounding areas not only economically but also socially and politically.

In these ways the preindustrial city in America functioned as a complex and diverse organizing element in American life, not as a simple, homogeneous, and static unit. The dynamic force of these early cities

1 and 2   Above, Philadelphia in 1702. By 1790, at the first census, it had a population of 54,000 and was America's second largest city. Below, Broadway in New York about 1830, when it was still a "walking" city.

3 Scene in early-nineteenth-century Philadelphia, its most prominent feature, Franklin House, a hotel typical of the period.

was reinforced by the nature of their setting and by the process of town diffusion. Throughout the preindustrial period of American history the cities occupied sites on the eastern portion of the largely undeveloped and richly endowed continent, and the settlement of countryside was generally preceded by the planting of towns in that region. The various interests in each city tended to compete with their counterparts in other cities for economic, social, and political control first of nearby and later of more distant and larger territories. And always there remained the virgin areas to be penetrated through the establishment of new towns by individuals and groups seeking economic opportunities or a more congenial social, political, or religious atmosphere. In this sense the cities spearheaded the development of a succession of urban frontiers. The conflicting "urban imperialism" of competing cities provided much of the drive behind the expansionist impulse in early American history. Mercantile and civic leaders felt that they must relentlessly "boost" their cities in order to attract the economic and other institutions upon which survival and growth in the interurban struggle seemed to depend.

6

While this set of circumstances made Americans one of the most prolific and self-conscious city-building peoples of their time, it did not result in a steadily urbanizing society in the sense that decade by decade an ever larger proportion of the population lived in cities. In 1690 an estimated 9 to 10 percent of American colonists lived in urban settlements. A century later, though 24 places numbered 2500 persons or more, city dwellers accounted for only 5.1 percent of the total population. For the next thirty years the proportion remained relatively stable, and it was 1830 before the urban figure moved back up to the level of 1690. In short, as the number of cities increased after 1690 they channeled larger numbers of people into the countryside than they retained. Nonetheless, the incessant movement of diverse people into and out of the cities made life in the many but relatively small places lively, stimulating, and mutable.

NEW FORMS: THE PROVINCIAL AMERICAN

Huddled in or near small though flourishing towns on the initial urban frontier, the first generation of settlers eagerly anticipated the emergence of social, political, and religious forms common to their past experience. But the diverse origins of the first generation, the continued influx of newcomers who had different backgrounds in England, and the splitting of old towns and planting of new ones prevented early colonial urban society from settling into a common and familiar mold. Hence, between 1680 and 1740 the towns experienced a critical transition, during which doubts were raised about the role of the cities in the imperial scheme of things and there was uncertainty, fear, and confusion about the social structure that might emerge in the New World. Though the turmoil did not produce a revolution, increasingly after the turn of the century growing numbers of urbanites came to regard themselves as provincial Americans rather than colonial Englishmen. They now seemed more inclined to loosen imperial restraints on their economic endeavors and political activities, and less inclined to model their social structure after Engish patterns.

Several factors generated this fundamental transformation in attitudes. Between 1680 and 1740 the populations of New York, Newport,

Philadelphia, and Charleston more than tripled; Boston's more than doubled; and merchants and other special interest groups in each place intensified their efforts to expand their immediate hinterlands. At the same time a host of secondary cities challenged the older places for regional leadership. Out of the growing commerce that this competition produced emerged (1) a class of moderately prosperous merchants in each of the major cities whose status rested more on their wealth than on their nobility or religious affiliations, (2) a larger number of artisans and mechanics who provided the skills and goods necessary to sustain an economy based on shipping, and (3) a set of professionals who supplied the educational, legal, religious, and informational needs of the busy and expanding commercial communities. The simultaneous emergence, moreover, of second- and third-generation native-born American city dwellers inexperienced in European ways, the immigration of Scotch-Irish, German, French Huguenot, and Jewish settlers, and the importation of black slaves provided the setting for an increase in the rate of physical and social mobility. With the growth and diversification of the population and expansion of the economy came serious problems of poverty and crime and widespread confusion about the place, status, and role of the various ethnic, religious, and socioeconomic groups. Among a people long conditioned to a hierarchical and rigid social system there had evolved a very un-English society in which no one knew his place. As one historian put it, "The unrest reflected the insecurity of every man. No one, irrespective of his success, was assured of his present status, much less of his future status."[1]

The pervasive unease that arose from these unsettled conditions expressed itself in a series of "revolts" and other manifestations, including witch hunts in Salem and anti-Catholic and anti-black outbreaks in New York—incidents that stemmed not so much from conflicts between clearly defined groups as from the general sense of social dislocation.

THE PROVINCIAL PERIOD

About 1740 this fluid turn-of-the-century urban society gave way to a more clearly defined socioeconomic milieu and a growing acceptance of the fact that social patterns in the cities of the New World differed from those of the Old. By mid-century the process of adjusting to new conditions was completed and the provincial period in colonial history had begun.

The new era was characterized in the first place by a more clearly defined pattern of urban dominance. By 1750 Boston, Newport, New York, Philadelphia, and Charleston had turned back the challenges of the secondary towns and now clearly dominated the urban system. The five major cities were not only larger than their competitors, but their influence extended over broader areas. In this view the thirteen British colonies in North America can be viewed as divided into five city-centered regions, each focused on a major port. Though Boston occupied the apex of the urban hierarchy and functioned, through its superior communications network among places on both sides of the Atlantic, as the coordinating element in the system, all of the cities

4   Port activities on New York's South Street in 1828.

served as corridors between the interior and the Old World. Increasingly, and despite British policy to the contrary, manufacturing for export to domestic markets became an important part of each city's economy. People, goods, and ideas, then, flowed between the provincial cities, between them and the surrounding countryside, and through them, to and from Europe and the rest of the world.

Life in the five major towns contrasted sharply with that in other sections of the colonies. City dwellers had easier access to private and public educational institutions, and the close contact between the American ports and Europe opened the provincial towns to the most recent vogues in continental thought and fashion. These factors, combined with the social interaction rendered inevitable by the concentration of population and with the broadened point of view stemming from commercial expansion and material prosperity made urban society, as Carl Bridenbaugh has put it, "more cooperative and social, less individualistic in its outlook toward problems of daily life, far more susceptible to outside influences and example, less aggressively independent than the society of frontier America."[2] By the mid-eighteenth century, moreover, the urban social structure was more complex than that in the countryside and differed in significant ways from the European pattern. Still extremely fluid by Old World standards, it permitted enough economic and physical mobility to keep society in constant flux. (Nonetheless, the rate of movement up and down the scale had declined, and the demarcations between levels stood out more clearly than during the transitional period of the turn-of-the-century years.)

Emergence of an Elite

By 1750 socioeconomic elites in each city exercised a political influence disproportionate to their numbers. In every town but Charleston, power rested in the hands of the more prosperous merchants and a cadre of professionals frequently linked to the leading mercantile families by marriage as well as by economic and intellectual interests. Charleston differed only slightly. There the planters, half-time residents of the city, joined the leaders of Charleston's commercial enterprises to form the city's elite community. Wealthier and more skilled than other provin-

5 House-moving in turn-of-the-century (eighteenth) Philadelphia. The social fluidity of the time was reflected in the cities' physical bustle and flux.

cial politicians, the urban elites and their allies not only dominated domestic affairs, but by 1750 had also secured for many colonies a greater political autonomy within the empire. Everywhere these elites played a crucial part in strengthening assemblies and councils as a means of asserting provincial "rights" against the imperial authorities. In those provinces most isolated from the influence of a single major city—North Carolina, New Jersey, Virginia, Maryland, and New Hampshire—the rise of legislatures and increases in provincial autonomy lagged.

The political aggressiveness of the urban elites was merely one expression of the dynamism built into the structure of the mid- and late-eighteenth-century urban communities. Reflecting on their achievements, a wide range of provincial urbanites felt disinclined to assume a subordinate or inferior stance in comparison with other similar groups in Old World cities, and the close commercial contacts among the American ports, bolstered by interurban marriages and traveling, fed this spirit of independence and self-sufficiency. In addition, the new and seemingly stable mid-century urban socioeconomic structure contained the elements necessary for a volatile reaction in a period of

11

economic or political crisis. The upper classes cherished and carefully guarded the economic, social, and political prerogatives and privileges that accrued to them in the relative freedom of American urban society. Those who had recently arrived among the elite, or who harbored aspirations of reaching the pinnacle in the near future, resented any effort to freeze the social structure or block the access to upward mobility with obstacles unrelated to merit and the accumulation of wealth. A large class of propertied artisans, shopkeepers, and traders shared a similar concern about the prospects for economic mobility. And at the bottom of the scale the increasingly crowded ranks of seamen and laborers struggled to eke out a living. Despite the disparity in wealth among these groups, they shared an interest in the continued prosperity and growth of the cities. The stability of urban provincial society, in short, hung on the taut strings of commerce and manufacturing, and the power to manipulate those strings decisively rested, in the final analysis, in the hands of British ministers and legislators in London.

Conflict and Rivalry

As the last third of the eighteenth century began, city dwellers drifted into a belligerent mood. An intensification of urban rivalries placed an economic strain on the bigger centers. As early as 1750, Boston's mercantile community entered a period of long decline relative to Philadelphia's ascendancy. In addition, the secondary cities continued to press the major ones. Augusta and Savannah threatened Charleston; Norfolk and Annapolis challenged Philadelphia; Salem and Portsmouth contributed to Boston's difficulties; Providence began to eclipse Newport. With the conclusion of the French and Indian War in 1763 the tension mounted, for peace ushered in a period of rising expectations, uneven economic recovery, and a series of sharp disagreements with the imperial authorities.

Merchants in the major cities responded to the economic challenge by redoubling their efforts to develop, control, and enlarge the hinterlands that fed the commerce of their cities. Their success was reflected in the growing numbers of artisans and mechanics and the expanded manufacturing activities, which provided a broadened base of interest in the trade of the cities. As a result of these developments the larger cities grew and prospered, but to many townsmen the social as well as the economic rewards seemed unevenly distributed. The expanding middle classes, a broad and heterogeneous conglomeration of artisans, mechanics, and shopkeepers, felt that they were making important contributions to city life yet suffering inordinately from dislocations over which they had no control. They now began to demand, occasionally through mob violence, a larger influence in public affairs, and politicians in Boston, New York, and Newport took the lead in focusing these grievances and bringing them to light in a systematic way.

A series of disagreements with the imperial authorities deepened the discontent and directed it toward London. After 1763, in an effort to raise revenues to help offset the expenses of maintaining the Empire, British authorities sought to tighten their regulation of provincial commerce and to inhibit the growth of provincial manufacturers who competed with those in England. Each new piece of legislation evoked protests centered in the cities, for each new tax or regulation bore on the townsmen with special force. The Sugar Act of 1764 struck at the traditional practice, lucrative in the long run, of bribing customs officials in the ports. The Stamp Act of 1765 came down hard on urban lawyers and printers by imposing taxes on legal documents, newspapers, and almanacs. The Townshend Act, which levied taxes on building materials such as glass, lead, and paint, struck with special intensity at the artisans and mechanics of the cities during a period of rapid urban expansion and housing shortages.

The crisis in the cities mounted steadily. When peaceful opposition through legal channels failed to secure relief, carefully organized bands of protestors, like the Sons of Liberty, used violence to intimidate the British officials responsible for enforcing the laws. The movement of British troops into the cities to secure order made matters worse. Moonlighting soldiers competed for jobs with townsmen, and the troops' off-duty recreational activities, particularly their womanizing, incensed a wide range of city dwellers. In addition, the uniforms of the soldiery made them conspicuous and inviting targets for youthful gangs. In this context the Boston Massacre of 1770 represented only the most violent incident in a protracted guerilla warfare between urban protesters and the authorities.

The imperial crisis climaxed in Boston. With the city's old supremacy eroded, leaders there desperately resisted every obstacle restricting their economic endeavors and political significance. The Boston Port Act of 1772 and the Massachusetts Government Act of 1774 proved too much. The latter limited town meetings to one per year, except by permission of the governor, and authorized army commanders to quarter troops in private homes rather than in barracks. The Port Act not only closed the port for shipping until restitution had been paid for a tea cargo that militants had dumped into the harbor, but also required all cargoes of wood bound for Boston to be unloaded and reloaded at Marblehead, a stipulation that increased the already high price of fuel in a city subject to intensely cold winters. That hurt everyone, especially the lower classes, and the intensity of the reaction became obvious when, after hostilities erupted, colonial forces cut off the supply of wood and forced the British troops and Tories within the city to burn fences, trees, and parts of buildings to warm themselves.

In this perspective the Revolution had its roots in the cities, and Boston played a particularly important role in the movement for inde-

WILLIAM JACKSON,

an *IMPORTER*; at the

BRAZEN HEAD,

North Side of the TOWN-HOUSE,

and *Oppoſite the Town-Pump, i*

Corn-hill, BOSTON.

6 Agitation against British economic and political restrictions: a pre-revolution handbill of the Sons and Daughters of Liberty calls for boycott of an uncooperative importer.

It is deſired that the SONS and DAUGHTERS of *LIBERTY,* would not buy any one thing of him, for in ſo doing they will bring Diſgrace upon *themſelves,* and their *Poſterity,* for *ever* and *ever,* AMEN.

7 Rural support of urban resistance to British domination of the colonies: a "stamp master" is hanged in effigy in New Hampshire.

pendence. After the coercive legislation of 1774, Massachusetts' chief city revolted, called for help, and discovered that the process of urbanization in the eighteenth century had produced in the other towns powerful groups that were not only different from the British, and knew it, but that also understood the broader implications of the conflict in Boston. Accusing the King and Parliament of subverting self-evident provincial rights, the urban politicians carried the cities and the countryside with them in a drive to oppose the tightening of imperial restraints and to preserve a society unshackled by the aristocratic forms of the past. Negotiations, accompanied by sporadic fighting, persisted into 1776. But then the British balked, and the cry for provincial rights emerged as a cry for American rights. Though less than 5 percent of the population was urban, it was in the cities that the coincidence of people, events, ideas, and leadership forged both a sense of American nationalism and a revolution.

The Cities and the Federal System

The cities became, of course, major strategic targets during the war, and some of them suffered serious damage. Yet they recovered rapidly, despite a brief recession in the 1780s. After the war urban politicians

15

took the lead in replacing the Articles of Confederation with a stronger central government. City-based delegates dominated the Constitutional Convention of 1787, and 87 percent of the members from the crucial states of New York, Massachusetts, Pennsylvania, and Virginia had significant urban experiences or connections. In the struggle for ratification, moreover, every city, regardless of its sectional location, voted for the Constitution. Ratification celebrations, like that in Norfolk, turned out representatives of virtually every occupational group. Combined, these events underscore the nationalizing influence of urban life, illustrate the striking homogeneity of economic interest among diverse groups in the commercial communities, and suggest that city dwellers accustomed to active municipal governments were less fearful of central governmental power than individuals who lived in scattered settlements across the countryside.

In the first few decades of its existence the new federal system of government was subjected to serious stress, and some of the discontent was traceable to the fluctuating pace of urban growth. Between 1790 and 1815 the older and larger cities north of the Potomac stagnated as English discrimination and a series of wars in Europe associated with the French Revolution and the ascendancy of Napoleon narrowed the range of trade opportunities in the familiar channels. For the first time new urban formation on the northeastern seaboard virtually ceased. Other cities also suffered, and between 1810 and 1820 the urban proportion of the nation's population dropped. But those places that, like Boston and other urban centers in New England, had a limited hinterland underwent the most strain. In the first decade and a half of the nineteenth century their spokesmen repeatedly threatened extreme action, including secession, and probed for new markets in Africa and Asia as they frantically sought a way out of their restricted economic circumstances.

NEW GROWTH AND NEW CONFLICTS

Although the rate of urbanization slackened between 1810 and 1820, the groundwork was being laid for a new burst of urban growth. The merchants and financiers of New York played a critical part in this

8 Comment on Boston's threat to surrounding towns. The caption reads: "The insatiate monster BOSTON, devouring the small cities, towns, villages, etc."

development. Unlike other major ports, New York after 1817 eliminated two sets of middlemen from the trans-Atlantic trade by permitting British manufacturers to consign their goods directly to auctioneers for sale on this side of the ocean. The object was to make all the Atlantic cities tributary to New York. That same year New York merchants became the first to establish a regularly scheduled shipping service, initially in the trans-Atlantic and eventually in the coastal trade all the way down to New Orleans. These innovations played a key role in vaulting the New York area to the top of the urban hierarchy with a population of about one million by 1860 (including that of Brooklyn, at the time a politically autonomous entity).

Competition and Cooperation

The Boston, Philadelphia, and Baltimore mercantile communities tried to compete with New York, but met with less success than the

17

9 Canal boats passing through mid-nineteenth-century Rochester in upstate New York.

latter. Beginning about 1820 canals and railroads comprised the chief instruments of conflict, and the fight centered on efforts to tap the commerce of the interior. New York reached toward the old Northwest by starting construction of the Erie Canal along the Great Lakes route. Philadelphia interests led the drive that culminated in the creation of the Pennsylvania canal system and even tried to throw a canal up and over the Appalachian Mountains. But the commercial leaders of Baltimore, perhaps encouraged by the exuberant growth of their city in the early nineteenth century, opted for trying to adapt the newly invented steam railroad to long-haul traffic. It worked. Though the Baltimore & Ohio Railroad did not enable Baltimore to outstrip either New York or Philadelphia in the decennial census statistics, it did help Baltimore achieve and retain a third-place rank until after 1860. By the mid-nineteenth century urban imperialists everywhere were turning to the railroad.

18

Well before the fruition of these schemes to control the commerce of the old Northwest, however, another urban frontier had taken shape. In the late eighteenth and increasingly in the early nineteenth century, settlers and explorers struggled along paths and crude roads and floated down the Ohio River into the new country. By 1800 surveyors and settlers had already cleared and laid out the sites of every major city in the Ohio Valley and lower Great Lakes region but Chicago, Indianapolis, and Milwaukee. Between 1790 and 1820 Pittsburgh, Lexington, Cincinnati, Louisville, St. Louis, Detroit, Buffalo, and Cleveland struggled successfully for control of their hinterlands with nearby rivals.

The new communities, moreover, quickly displayed a stratified social and political structure and cooperative civic spirit that set them off from

10   A sectional canal boat in Philadelphia in 1840. The boats (with passengers) were hauled by wagon through the city, then by train to the Pennsylvania Canal, where they were joined to other boat sections, their ultimate destination Pittsburgh.

11 An eighteenth-century factory—the Salem Iron Factory—in Salem, Massachusetts.

the countryside, just as the urban East and South contrasted with the rural. Not surprisingly, city-based western congressmen and senators, working within the national two-party structure, found that they had common ground with some of their eastern and southern colleagues on which to build an "American system." With the aim of stimulating commerce and manufacturing throughout the country, spokesmen for this outlook advocated a national currency, federal spending to improve the internal transportation system, and a protective tariff. One of them, President James Madison, had, since the 1780s, sought to foster urban interests, for after that time Norfolk, Richmond, and other towns in his native state of Virginia lagged seriously in the urban imperialist contest. Another, Henry Clay, came from Kentucky and felt compelled to promote the interests of his supporters in the important cities of Louisville and Lexington. A third, John Adams, of Massachusetts and Boston, represented an even larger urban constituency, and John Calhoun, of South Carolina, for a time supported this kind of program in part to protect the declining fortunes of Charleston. Through the "American system," in short, the cities functioned as nationalizing

20

agents that helped hold together a country of growing regional diversity.

After 1830, however, the acrid competition for control of the commerce of the interior resumed, continuing to pit old cities against new and section against section. Though this contest eventually produced a transportation network that drew eastern and western cities closer, it also contributed to the growing spirit of resentment and sectional separatism in the South by cutting Dixie off from the major commercial routes. New Orleans and St. Louis relied primarily and for too long on their old ally, the Mississippi river, while to the east, where older cities continued their fight for advantage in the western trade, powerful men supported the construction of railroads. Slowly, major trunk lines anchored in New York, Philadelphia, and Baltimore pushed toward the core of the continent. In the West, Chicago business leaders grasped the chance, making connections to nearby centers and pushing lines out over the prairies. By 1860 the cities of the West were bound to those in the East by steel and steam as well as by canals, and New Orleans, like other southern centers, had entered a period of relative decline as the new transportation network deflected movement of the produce of the West from its traditional north-south axis onto an east-west plane. In this context the secession of the South represented an attempt to break out of the economic straitjacket imposed upon the region by the appearance of a new national system of cities that centered diversified economic growth in the East and old Northwest.

SUMMARY

Clearly, cities in the preindustrial era played an important role in early American history. In the seventeenth century they served as initial settlements that secured a beachhead for colonists, and the intense competition among seaboard cities generated an expansive impulse that fostered economic growth and cultural development. During the critical years of the late eighteenth and early nineteenth centuries cities functioned as nationalizing agents that first sparked the drive for independence and then helped hold the new nation together. After 1820 urban imperialism fostered the adoption of transportation innovations and quickened the westward movement, and the proliferation of cities in

12 and 13 Boston in 1722 *(above)* and in 1814 *(facing page)*.

the rich region west of the Appalachians and the forging of water and rail communications between eastern and western cities reduced the economic and political power of the South and revived the fires of sectional antagonism. By that time, however, both the preindustrial city and the commercial-agrarian society within which it flourished had begun to disintegrate. Basic changes in the structure of both the economy and cities after 1840 brought to an end the first era in American urban history and inaugurated a new period of unequaled urban growth and unprecedented turbulence.

22

Notes

[1] Clarence Ver Steeg, *The Formative Years, 1607–1763* (New York: Hill and Wang, 1964), p. 132.

[2] Carl Bridenbaugh, *Cities in the Wilderness* (New York: Knopf, 1938), p. 481.

Bibliography

Albion, Robert. *The Rise of New York Port, 1815–1860.* New York: Scribner, 1939. An older but nonetheless invaluable explanation of why New York rose to the top of the urban hierarchy in the first half of the nineteenth century.

Boorstin, Daniel J. *The Americans: The National Experience.* New York: Random House, 1965. Though not an urban history, this volume points up the influence of urban settlements in the early period of United States history. The material on "boosters" is especially illuminating.

Bridenbaugh, Carl. *Cities in Revolt: Urban Life in America, 1743–1776.* New York: Capricorn Books, 1964. An important book that clearly demonstrates the point that cities exercise an influence disproportionate to their numbers and size. Also effectively conveys the texture of early American urban life.

Greene, Jack P. "The Role of the Lower Houses of Assembly in Eighteenth Century Politics." *Journal of Southern History.* XXVII (Nov., 1961), 451–74. Implies a close relationship between urbanization and the rise of the lower legislative houses.

Henratta, James A. "Economic Development and Social Structure in Colonial Boston." *The William and Mary Quarterly,* 3rd sec. (January 22, 1965), 75–92. Analyzes changes in social structure wrought by economic growth in Boston during the late seventeenth and eighteenth centuries.

Lockridge, Kenneth A. *A New England Town: The First Hundred Years.* New York: Norton, 1970. One of a series of recent and very excellent monographs on the internal conflict and instability of early towns. Emphasizes the cohesion of early settlements, but also helps explain the breakdown of seventeenth-century social and geographic patterns.

Miller, Zane L. "Daniel Drake, the City, and the American System," in Henry D. Shapiro and Zane L. Miller, eds., *Physician to the West: Selected Writings of Dr. Daniel Drake on Science and Society.* Lexington: The Univ. Press of Kentucky, 1970. Examines the ideas and activities of one exponent of the critical role of cities in the "American system."

Powell, Sumner Chilton. *Puritan Village: The Formation of a New England Town.* Garden City, N.Y.: Doubleday, 1965. A Pulitzer-prize-winning account of the ways in which English migrants improvised new societies in America.

Rubin, Julius. "Growth and Expansion of Urban Centers," in David T. Gilchrist, ed., *The Growth of Seaport Cities, 1790–1825.* Charlottesville: The Univ. Press of Virginia, 1967. An important essay on the relationship between the structure of towns in the early nineteenth century and differential economic development by region.

Taylor, George R. *The Transportation Revolution, 1815–1860.* New York: Harper, 1968. Underplays the dynamic role of cities in economic growth, but is important for its exploration of the close connection between transportation innovations, the growth of cities, and economic development.

Wade, Richard C. *The Urban Frontier: Pioneer Life in Early Pittsburgh, Cincinnati, Lexington, Louisville, and St. Louis.* Chicago: The Univ. of Chicago Press, 1964. The most concise and readable presentation of the urban frontier thesis.

The Mid- 2
Nineteenth-Century
Urban Explosion

Most Americans of the post-1945 generation associate the idea of "urban explosion" with the 1950s and 1960s. Purveyors of the concept used it as a convenient shorthand with which to sum up a variety of startling and seemingly uncontrollable developments, most notably a mushroom growth of the urban population, a dramatic expansion in the physical dimensions of cities, and an upsurge in crime and violence. Few, however, suggested that the nation might have experienced earlier urban explosions. The transitional years of the colonial period, for example, might well bear such a label, as could the era of the American Revolution. Yet a more persuasive case can be made for the proposition that the mid-nineteenth century deserves recognition as the era of the first and perhaps the most severe urban explosion in American history, for in these years the United States urbanized at a rate never before or since matched. Between 1820 and 1860 the western edge of the urban frontier leapfrogged from the Mississippi to California, and the proportion of people living in cities jumped by 797 percent while the population of the nation increased by a comparatively meager 226 percent. The burst of city growth peaked in the two decades immediately preceding the Civil War. The urban proportion of the population went up by 92.1 percent in the 1840s and 75.4 percent in the 1850s, while the total population of the nation rose by only 35.9 and 35.6 percent, respectively. Twenty years before 1840 only 12 cities exceeded 10,000 inhabitants, and but two were greater than 100,000. Twenty years after 1840, 101 cities numbered more than 10,000 people, 8 held over 100,000, and New York had already hit the 1,000,000 mark.

Economic, geographic, social, and political events also mark the middle decades of the nineteenth century as an explosive phase in American urban history. By 1860 five of the fifteen most densely populated areas listed more than 10 percent of their total populations employed in manufacturing, a clear indication that large-scale urban growth no longer depended so heavily on commerce. After 1840, moreover, the cities began to expand physically. In the late eighteenth century the radius of settlement seldom exceeded one mile; by the midnineteenth century it more commonly ran to four or five. Finally, as the restricted casements of the preindustrial walking city stretched, city dwellers found themselves caught up in an environment plagued by appallingly high levels of violence, poverty, congestion, disease, mortality, and governmental and political ineptitude. The new intensity of these problems, the rise of manufacturing, and the expansion of cities in physical size and population indicated that by 1840 the first phase in the creation of a new kind of city and of an industrial nation had begun.

INDUSTRIALIZATION

The Transportation-Communication Network

The beginnings of industrialization in any society derive from a variety of sources, but recent analyses of the process in the United States suggest that one factor acted as the critical catalyst. Although the

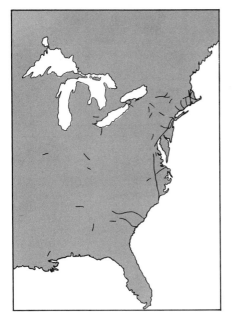

14   Growth of railroad lines in the mid-nineteenth century. At left, their extent
in 1840, and, at right, ten years later.

national railway network that was completed between 1840 and 1880
has often been depicted as the dynamic element in the entrance of the
United States into the first stage of industrialization, it was interurban
rivalries that first provided the major impetus for the creation of that
railroad system. With few exceptions most early railroads were originally projected as short-run lines to tap and develop the immediate hinterlands of particular cities. In the second quarter of the nineteenth
century, however, cities east of the Mississippi took the lead in constructing long-run lines to tie them more closely to the cities of the
interior and to the entrepôts of the deep South, Southwest, and the West
Coast, and cities around the edge of the continent and urban places in
the interior soon joined the push.

Before the Civil War, however, the railroad movement began to focus
on the need for transcontinental truck lines. Growth of urban-based
sentiment in favor of transcontinental projects facilitated the passage by
Congress of the Pacific Railways Acts of 1862 and 1864. This legislation
authorized generous subsidies for railway construction and set off

27

15 and 16 At left, Illinois Central tracks on the outskirts of Chicago in 1866, and, below, part of an offering for sale of lands along the Central's right-of-way.

ILLINOIS CENTRAL RAILROAD COMPANY

OFFER FOR SALE

ONE MILLION ACRES OF SUPERIOR FARMING LANDS,

IN FARMS OF

40, 80 & 160 acres and upwards at from $8 to $12 per acre.

THESE LANDS ARE

NOT SURPASSED BY ANY IN THE WORLD.

THEY LIE ALONG

THE WHOLE LINE OF THE CENTRAL ILLINOIS RAILROAD,

For Sale on LONG CREDIT, SHORT CREDIT and for CASH, they are situated near TOWNS, VILLAGES, SCHOOLS and CHURCHES.

intense competition among towns and cities across the country for connections with a cross-country line. The struggle in the trans-Mississippi West was particularly brutal and expensive. During the 1860s, for example, Kansas City entrepreneurs underwrote the future growth of their city by persuading the Hannibal and St. Joseph Railroad to tie into the Union Pacific. Backers of the project had to float bond issues, secure a federal land grant, and put up blocks of potentially valuable real estate to finance the enterprise. Railroad promoters and boosters in Cheyenne, Denver, Reno, Tacoma, and a host of other places used similar techniques to provide a lifeline for the future growth of their cities. Losers in these battles, like Parkville, Missouri, and Auraria, Colorado, remained obscure villages or disappeared entirely. But the disadvantages of this interurban rivalry reached beyond localities, for the demand of cities for spots on the vital transcontinental links was so strenuous that the national railway system was overbuilt and often shoddily constructed. Moreover, the cutthroat competition that developed among these essentially weak railroads created periodic fiscal havoc among railway financiers, which helped trigger the depression of 1873. Yet none of these economic difficulties bore sufficient impact to impede railway construction seriously, and by 1880 the outlines of the modern railway network were already etched on the map of America.

As in the earlier canal stage of transportation development, the urban imperialists of the railroad era raised much of the money for the work, led the political battles for subsidies and the granting of rights-of-way, selected the routes, and reaped the greatest profits. Cities across the country boomed as the national system of railroads filled out. Not only did the older cities of the East Coast, Ohio Valley, and Great Lakes region benefit from trading in the wider markets opened by railroad expansion, but younger towns mushroomed as well. For the first time, too, the South experienced significant urban growth within the ring of major cities that dotted the periphery of the section in the early nineteenth century. Atlanta began its rise to regional hegemony in the Southeast after the Civil War, and in the same years railroad promoters and real estate speculators launched Birmingham, Alabama, and dubbed it the "Magic City" of Dixie as its population and industrial productivity exploded in the late 1870s and early 1880s.

But the impact of railroad construction was most dramatic in the West. The vast territory between the Mississippi and the Rockies ranked as the most rapidly urbanizing section of the country in the latter years of this period, and there the relationship between city rivalries, railroads, urbanization on the frontier, and the process of settlement and economic and cultural development could be seen most clearly. First the railroads that pushed out from eastern cities touched and vitalized isolated mining camps, trading villages, and cattle towns. Then new places sprang up along the route, and finally came the farms. Because of this sequence, noted one contemporary observer, "the city stamps the country. . . . It is the cities and towns which will frame state constitutions, make laws, create public opinion, establish social usages, and fix standards of morals in the West."[1]

17   Commodore Vanderbilt and Jim Fisk, heads of their respective railroad lines, jockey for position in the race to open up—and secure dominance in—the vast territories of the West.

THE GREAT RACE FOR THE WESTERN STAKES 1870

Development of Large-Scale Manufacturing

The appearance of a new national transportation system between 1840 and 1880 also created conditions that stimulated the organization of large-scale manufacturing and, for the first time, made the factory an integral part of the urban economic and geographic structure. Filling out of the national railroad network and the spread of telegraph and telephone lines that accompanied it cut the costs of production by reducing the expense of shipping both raw materials and finished goods. At the same time, the new transportation-communications system, by accelerating the growth of cities and opening new territory for agricultural development, produced vast new urban and rural markets, which intensified demands for consumer goods such as salt, sugar, leather, whiskey, starch, flour, biscuit, clothing, and footwear.

The reduced costs of transportation and enlarged markets also provided strong incentives for managerial and manufacturing innovations. The response to the new conditions, however, did not have a homogenizing effect on the organization of production in cities. Entrepreneurs reacted so variously that by 1860 the manufacturing profile of any big city appeared to be a hodgepodge of large and small enterprises practicing diverse production methods in a broad range of organizational schemes. In 1874, for example, several leading firms in the rubber boot, shoe, and glove industries formed the Associated Rubber Shoe Companies, which, through its board of directors, set price and production schedules. About the same time, James B. Duke laid the groundwork for the American Tobacco Company by applying machinery to the production of cigarettes. His product sold almost exclusively in cities, and he soon moved his base of marketing and distribution operations from Durham, North Carolina, to New York City, the one place in which he could command the communications links and financial resources necessary to secure access to an urban "hinterland" of continental proportions. Gustavus Swift, a Chicago meat packer, moved in yet another direction. After experimenting successfully with the refrigerated railroad car, he built plants in several cities that packed and distributed fresh meat to urban markets across the country. Size, in short, was about the only thing common to these enterprises.

It is important to recognize, however, that the wave of business innovation in the consumer goods industries involved neither a whole-sale adoption of large and well-coordinated marketing, distribution, pricing, or production schemes, nor an instant conversion to factory methods of production everywhere and in all lines of manufacture. More commonly, hard-pressed master artisans and mechanics seeking to enlarge their output intensified the division of labor by divorcing themselves from the task of producing goods and moving into a co-ordinating role. From this position they parceled out the job on a piece-meal basis to individuals or to groups of five to twenty semiskilled workers who completed one part or another of an item and passed it on to the next link in the production chain. Well before 1880, this kind of small shop had emerged as the characteristic mode of consumer goods production in American big cities, eclipsing craftsmen-retailers work-ing alone or with one or two apprentices. But as early as 1860 these shops, in turn, were increasingly giving way to factories, in which all the tasks performed in the manufacture of a finished product took place under one roof.

Most of the largest factories appeared in the producers' goods indus-try, a new line of endeavor that grew as an adjunct to the emerging transportation-communications system. The construction of long-run railroads and intercity telegraph and telephone lines required large amounts of iron and steel for rolling stock, rails, and bridges, and an increased supply of copper for wire and other electrical equipment. These producers' goods industries, so-called because their products were not absorbed directly by the ultimate consumer, relied heavily on mass production techniques in large shops and factories. Some of them, like the Baldwin locomotive plant in Philadelphia, which employed as many as 600 workers, were truly massive operations.

The growing practice of assembling large numbers of workers at one site within cities made the factory for the first time a typically urban institution. Before 1840, factories had usually been located along rela-tively isolated water power sites, though a few could be found scattered around the periphery of those towns and cities that developed on land adjacent to rapidly running water or that built "races" through which water was run for the propulsion of machinery. But the new demand for manufactured goods led to the increasing use of steam power, which,

18 Typical nineteenth-century producer's-goods industry: a Massachusetts forgings plant.

since it could be generated almost anywhere, permitted location of factories on almost any site. Plant managers, however, preferred big cities to bucolic villages, and for good reasons. In the cities they could take advantage of large and therefore relatively cheap pools of labor and utilize, at no expense of their own, transportation networks reaching into regional and national raw-materials and consumer markets. In addition, the heterogeneous occupational structure of cities assured the manufacturers access to the multiplicity of allied services, including the legal talent, banking and repair facilities, and raw-materials processors required to supply, maintain, and manage the growing and complex enterprises.

As a consequence of the increasing size, diversity, and number of urban production units, manufacturing became an increasingly significant determinant of the occupational structure of cities. To be sure, in 1850 important and growing commercial centers such as New Orleans and San Francisco still had less than 3 percent of their residents engaged in manufacturing. But in older and larger places, such as Providence or Cincinnati, the figures ran from 10 to 20 percent; in the newer and smaller towns, such as Lowell and Lynn, Massachusetts, as high as 45 percent. But even though the percentages continued to mount during the 1860s and 1870s, the national economy remained essentially commercial and agrarian, for most of the urban manufacturers still only processed raw materials or agricultural goods for domestic or foreign markets.

Though the rising importance of manufacturing did not transform the character of the national economy, the broadening of job opportunities in cities, associated with the enlarged scale of manufacturing and the appearance of the factory, helps explain the disproportionately rapid growth of urban (as opposed to rural) populations between 1840 and 1880. Over that span of years the urban proportion of the total population rose from 11 to 28 percent, an average increase of about 4 percent per decade, and the total number of people living in cities jumped from 1,845,000 to 14,129,000. Little of the increment in the urban population stemmed from natural increase; most came from the influx of rural population, in part lured out of the countryside by the opportunities that came with urban economic diversification.

19   A clothing factory of about 1860.

20 Two prime movers of the agricultural revolution, a steam-driven tractor and power supply *(above)* and a mechanical thresher *(below)*.

THE AGRICULTURAL REVOLUTION:
THE MOVE FROM THE FARM

Apart from the pull of urban economic opportunities or, for that matter, the attraction of good times and bright lights in the cities, the rural-urban drift drew strength from "push" factors that drove people off the farms. These push factors grew out of the agricultural revolution, which, like the creation of the national railway system and the rise of manufacturing, was stimulated by the dissemination, growth, and spreading influence of cities. The mid-nineteenth-century urban network and transportation-communications web not only fed people into the rural areas but also facilitated the adoption of new farming methods that progressively reduced the need for farm labor. Because cities functioned as crucibles of technological and managerial innovation and as centers of marketing and information distribution operations, they moved not only people, but ideas and new technologies. The West, for example, was dotted with small- and medium-sized urban places closely tied to big cities—such as Chicago and St. Louis—by railroads, newspapers, farm journals, and traveling salesmen. Through these contacts farmers working unprecedentedly large acreages found it easy to keep up with and procure the latest equipment. The application of new technology, such as improved plows and the reaper, halved the time and labor cost of production. Fewer farmers and fewer farm laborers were now required to plant and harvest crops, and the superfluous agricultural workers were "pushed" toward the cities.

Although the demographic consequences of the agricultural revolution were felt most sharply after 1860 in the West, important changes in agricultural practice that produced similar net results began about a decade earlier east of the Mississippi and north of the Mason-Dixon line. Here, too, cities played a critical role. Though located in the emerging urban-industrial heartland, cities in this region still processed and distributed agricultural produce on a significant scale. As a consequence urban entrepreneurs had a large stake in stimulating productivity on the smaller farms that predominated in their hinterlands. As city populations increased and demand for foodstuffs grew, consumer goods businessmen took a strong interest in developing and disseminating information about new farming techniques and methods. Here,

21   The McCormick reaper, one of the farm machines that revolutionized agriculture in the mid-nineteenth century. The parts were labeled and numbered to simplify assembly by the farmer.

however, the special emphasis fell less on technology and more heavily on new methods of farm management, dairy cattle and hog breeding, insect and disease control, fertilization, plant hybridization, and food preservation. Information radiating from the cities by way of farm journals, newspapers, and traveling salesmen, in short, introduced "scientific" farming into these older farm areas. Like the new farm technology on the Plains, the advent of scientific farming boosted agricultural productivity markedly in the eastern half of the nation. The agricultural revolution on both sides of the Mississippi, though differing in thrust, nonetheless enabled fewer farmers to raise more food, released surplus rural population for urban life, and provided enough food to sustain the nation's burgeoning city population.

IMMIGRATION

Yet not all the new urban population came from rural America. During the 1840s crop failures in Europe set off a surge of emigration from Ireland, southwestern Germany, and Scandinavia. In the 1850s some 2,750,000 immigrants landed in the United States. The pace increased after the Civil War and peaked in 1873, when 400,000 newcomers

22   Mealtime on a ship bringing immigrants to the United States in 1870.

landed in American ports. Following a lull during the depression years of the middle and late 1870s, the movement resumed and reached unprecedented volume in the 1880s.

During the first twenty years of this influx most immigrants, but especially the desperately poor and unskilled rural Irish, remained in the city of their arrival. But as the railroad network took shape after the 1850s more and more northern Europeans filtered through Boston, New York, New Orleans, and other ports of entry into interior agricultural districts and urban centers, though relatively fewer remained in the South than before. Larger numbers of Scandinavians and Germans settled on farms, while the bulk of the newcomers continued to become city dwellers, and concentrated in the major manufacturing centers. By 1870 the Northeast contained almost 75 percent of the nation's foreign-born residents; in those sections of the country where manufacturing was less important the proportions ran much lower: the West Central region claimed 12.2 percent of the total; the South, 7.2 percent; the Mountain states, 1.4 percent; and the Pacific region, 3.1 percent.

Just as striking as the international and rural-to-urban flow of population in the mid-nineteenth century was the overall movement into and out of cities. A few recent studies indicate that the population of industrializing walking cities seemed to be constantly shifting. In these years the population turnover—that is, the sum of all movements into an area (including births) and all outward movements (including deaths)—reached an annual rate of at least 30 percent, well above the standard estimate of 20 percent for mid-twentieth-century America; furthermore, the rate tended to increase after 1840. During the 1880s, for example, Boston's population grew by 65,000, but roughly 1,000,000 individuals moved through the city to produce that net gain. The turnover rate, to be sure, was not equal for all groups. Foreign-born moved more often than native, younger individuals more often than older, and poorer classes more often than wealthier. But the net result was an incredible churning of the population. The typical city dweller moved three times before settling someplace at middle age, and the more volatile elements scarcely settled anywhere.

Between 1840 and 1880, then, urbanization played a critical role in the first stage of transforming a preindustrial into an industrial society.

23 The (somewhat exaggerated) chaos of "moving day" in the city, about 1840. Most residential leases expired on the same day—April 30.

Urban rivalries draped the country with a national transportation-communications system that had profound effects on manufacturing, farming, and the distribution, composition, and fluidity of the population. At the same time, a new continental system of cities and a new economic geography appeared. In the Northeast the urban-industrial heartland took shape and firmly established itself as the pacemaker and commanding factor in the national economy. Cities in that region contained the heaviest concentrations of industry, offered the most attractive economic opportunities, and led the nation in adopting technological innovations such as the horse-drawn street railway. On the eastern rim of the heartland lay the older cities of the Atlantic seacoast. Once the commercial gateways to the expanding interior, these cities had accumulated capital in over two and a half centuries of mercantile enterprise that provided them (especially New York) with the resources to become the nation's most powerful financial centers and with an initial advantage in attracting and setting up industries. Major cities to the south and west functioned as regional and subregional centers. They organized their hinterlands, gathered and processed raw materials and

39

agricultural goods for transfer into the heartland, and received and re-shipped finished consumer products and producers' goods transported back to them from the country's urban-industrial core.

CHANGES IN FORM

The coincidence of the rise of manufacturing and the emergence of the urban-industrial heartland with the redistribution, diversification, and increased mobility of the population forced on city dwellers a need to adjust continually to new conditions of life. Their difficulties in adapting to this highly unstable socioeconomic environment were complicated by a simultaneous disruption of the familiar geography of cities. Over the centuries, and in a variety of cultures, large cities had tended to have a similar structure—a shape and arrangement determined by a common technological reality. Until the mid-nineteenth century city dwellers traveled by foot or in animal-drawn, wheeled vehicles that accommodated but a few passengers. The absence of any form of mass rapid transit meant that cities had to be compact enough for urbanites to walk through their daily routines. Largely for this reason those residential sites nearest the centers of power and activity were the most prized, and those most removed were the least desirable. In the preindustrial walking city, as a result, the wealthy lived near the center of town, close by the government buildings, churches, and major commercial facilities, and the poor were pushed out toward the periphery.

24   Broadway (New York City) traffic scene in the 1850s.

25   An early commuter train at the station in Stamford, Connecticut, about 1870.

The Street Railway and Commuter Train

During the early nineteenth century most American cities still conformed to this historic pattern. Then the omnibus, the short-run steam railroad, and the horse-drawn street railway (capable of carrying as many as twenty passengers) blurred the old arrangement. These more rapid modes of moving large numbers of people provided city dwellers with a new range of physical movement. As a result, cities began after 1840 to expand in physical size, and the rate of residential mobility within urban centers reached unprecedentedly high levels. While the availability of new transportation facilities did not entirely eliminate the historic social geography of the walking city, the enlarged scale and increased fluidity of urban life did loosen and alter the structure of cities. For the first time, large-scale commuting, central business districts, and peripheral residential neighborhoods that grew more rapidly than those near the core became hallmarks of American cities.

In these years the dormitory-suburb occupied by businessmen and   41

26 Scene at the Morgan Park station on the Chicago, Rock Island & Pacific railway, which linked Chicago and the suburb of Blue Island.

professionals who made the daily trek to and from work in the city first appeared. To be sure, members of the mercantile elite had built homes in exclusive outlying districts around eastern seaports during the eighteenth century, and many of the same class purchased country estates within a half-day's journey from their city homes and places of employment. The introduction between 1830 and 1850 of the mass transit facilities described above not only encouraged this trend and spread it to cities in other parts of the country, but also helped establish the practice of daily commuting between suburb and city. By 1848 an estimated 20 percent of Boston's businessmen traveled to work on steam railroads, and 118 of 208 passenger trains entering and leaving the city's seven major terminals served only stations within fifteen miles of central Boston. The suburbs of which these stations formed the nucleus were both isolated from one another and buffered by a band of open land from the expanding urban fringe of poor city dwellers.

Interspersed among these affluent suburban enclaves appeared relatively autonomous villages of the less well-to-do—people who had been

attracted to the region by the city, but had spilled out beyond its boundaries along plank roads, rivers, canals, or railroad lines. Blue Island, Illinois, a small railroad town some sixteen miles south of downtown Chicago, near the southern tip of Lake Michigan, was fairly typical of these places. It had a diverse occupational, ethnic, and social structure, and more than half of its gainfully employed residents worked and spent most of their leisure hours in the village. Many Blue Island boosters even dreamed that their town might someday outstrip Chicago in the race for regional supremacy. Yet Blue Islanders never in these years freed themselves from dependence upon Chicago for banking, quality medical care, and a variety of other special services. By 1880 the town's competition with Chicago had narrowed to a contest for commercial dominance in southern Cook County, and increasing numbers of Blue Islanders had joined the ranks of Chicago's commuter classes.

While the steam commuter train stimulated suburban growth several miles distant from the major cities, introduction of the horse-drawn street railway in the 1850s expanded the scope of contiguous settlement. 43

Until 1860 few cities supported more than one or two street railway lines, and those usually ran to established exclusive neighborhoods inside the city limits. The horsecars were slow, but because they stopped at regular intervals, penetrated deep into the heart of the city, moved smoothly and easily along rails, and offered low fares, they soon became the major form of intracity mass rapid transit.

Beginning in the late 1860s, the horsecars pushed through previously unsettled territory to points as far as four miles from the city center, a journey of 30 to 45 minutes. Most of these new lines originally ran to outlying hospitals, cemeteries, parks, or amusement resorts, and depended on weekend and holiday traffic for revenues. But housing soon developed around these outlying nodes of activity, and by 1880 the construction of single-family dwellings within a 5-minute walk along the lines had generated enough regular traffic to support commuter service. But the land between the main residential bands adjacent to the horsecar tracks did not fill in, and the prongs of settlement stretching into the countryside tended to give the major cities a star-shaped pattern.

The Central Business District

Another important mid-nineteenth-century change in urban structure took place in the centers of the big cities. Most of the larger cities now developed a new and more elaborate central business district. Clustered about the edge, near water and railway terminal facilities, stood warehouses, manufacturing shops, and a few factories; the core contained small groups of retail and wholesale stores, theaters, newspapers, banks and insurance companies, a few hotels, and a handful of churches and government buildings.

"Downtown" now focused the life of the city and surrounding districts in an unprecedented way. It not only attracted commuting businessmen and professionals, but also visitors, shoppers, and amusement seekers from the city and its nearby hinterland. In addition, the central business district also drew increasing numbers of workers from outlying wards, who now found employment in the core businesses and services and in the nearby industries. Indeed, in 1860, Philadelphia's principal downtown ward provided workplaces for one-quarter of the city's manufacturing workers, and according to the best available estimates, a sizable proportion of these 30,000 men, women, and children made daily treks downtown from another ward. While some of these factory hands and other downtown employees now established their residences closer to the central business district, the bulk of the lower-middle and poorer classes still occupied the urban fringe.

The new arrangement of city life dictated by the intensification of activities in or near downtown, the shifting location of job opportunities, and the opening of new intraurban routes of travel contributed to the astonishingly unsettled character of residential neighborhoods within cities. People now shifted residences incessantly. The general direction of the moves was toward the periphery, with outer residential wards of cities growing more rapidly than those near the center, but in a given year some people would move from the center to the periphery, others would merely change addresses within the center or the periphery, and still others would press into the core from the city's edges. In Boston during the 1840s, this internal flux plus intercity migration meant that some 40 percent of the population moved into different households annually, a figure that, together with other, albeit sketchy, evidence, ranks the mid-nineteenth-century generation of urbanites as the most mobile in American history.

THE SOCIAL GEOGRAPHY: URBAN CRISIS

Although mid-nineteenth-century cities seemed perpetually in motion, they nonetheless possessed a discernible social and economic geography. Despite the eternal flux, snapshots of urban structure of the time reveal a fairly clear pattern: except for the new central business districts and the suburbs dotting the countryside around the major places, it generally resembled the structure of the preindustrial more closely than that of the modern city. Close by the central business district the chief in-town residential neighborhoods of the affluent remained. Outside those was a circle of single- and multifamily dwellings for the middle classes, punctuated by corner shops, saloons, churches, and budding secondary business districts. On the periphery, among the slaughterhouses, tanneries, soap factories, breweries, grog shops, and small groceries, concentrated the poor and the unsuccessful, both native and foreign-born, black and white.

45

Yet, because of the high mobility of the population and the rapidly growing area of cities, this picture was shifting and blurred. Some of the poor, for example, could be found in every ward, and ethnic concentrations seldom exceeded 60 percent of the inhabitants in any specific district. A lag in constructing inexpensive housing helps explain this pattern of relative dispersal. Newcomers and the poor appeared in such numbers that they had to move into converted warehouses, abandoned mansions, and ramshackle shanties in back lots and alleys across the face of the city. Since large-scale industrialization and major urban expansion, which would have provided unskilled factory and construction labor for masses of workers, lay in the future, only a few jobs awaited the unskilled and unlettered newcomers. Their poverty not only prevented them from securing decent housing, but also overtaxed the limited charity, relief, and almshouse facilities and crowded the streets with peddlers, hungry men searching the city for jobs and shelter, and beggars.

27 Tenement dwellers try to escape the heat of a New York City summer in the 1880s.

The combination of high population mobility, widespread economic insecurity, and class, ethnic, racial, and neighborhood tensions constituted the major elements out of which the mid-nineteenth-century urban crisis emerged. As the blighted fringe expanded, pushing waves of poverty, disease, and grog shops into every section of the city, many native American white Protestants concluded that the ragged edges of the city housed an alien and dangerous population composed of chronically idle native whites, racially inferior blacks, and unassimilable foreigners—the latter, more often than not, attached to the Catholic church. What was in fact the most mobile segment of a generally unstable urban population now appeared to be permanent, alien, and ubiquitous. As it encroached on the limited supply of available jobs and living space it seemed to threaten the welfare of the entire city.

Group Violence

Recurring outbursts of group violence were the most spectacular product of this higher visibility and of the volatile mixture of cultures in the mid-nineteenth-century city. Contemporaries often described participants in the big-city riots as deluded individuals caught up in the frenzy of mob passions. Yet crowd psychology alone could not have produced so many outbreaks in so many places in such a brief period. Far from being insensate outbursts by irrational mobs, the riots stemmed from the frustrations developed by the ceaseless shifting of the urban social, economic, religious, ethnic, and geographic structure, by poverty in general and, in particular, by the intolerable housing conditions among the poor, and their consequent intense competition with the lower-middle classes for jobs and living space.

The *immediate* causes and chief victims of the riots varied. In the early 1840s, Protestant mobs launched a series of attacks on Catholic churches and convents in widely separated locations. During the 1850s the attempt of politicians to incorporate immigrants into the political process focused the wrath of nativist groups on the foreign-born. New Orleans in that decade acquired a national reputation for political rioting, and other places, like Louisville, where at least 22 died in one election affray, experienced similar outbreaks. Labor disputes also contributed to the mayhem. The great railroad strike during the summer of

28 Strikers burn cars of the Pennsylvania Railroad near Pittsburgh in 1877.

1877 ignited pitched battles in cities across the country, including Baltimore, Philadelphia, Buffalo, Cleveland, Toledo, Columbus, Louisville, Indianapolis, Chicago, St. Louis, Kansas City, Omaha, and San Francisco. Casualties ran high in all these places, but Pittsburgh suffered most. In two days of fighting there, 15 soldiers and 50 workers were killed; and 500 freight cars, 104 steam locomotives, and 39 buildings were destroyed.

Though no one was wholly exempt from the riots, black city dwellers bore the brunt of urban group violence between 1840 and 1860. Philadelphia alone experienced five antiblack outbreaks between 1832 and 1849, Cincinnati its second in 1841 and another in 1863, and New York the bloodiest of all during the so-called draft riot of 1863. All of these incidents were initiated by whites, and in almost every case the riot climaxed with an assault on black residential quarters by white mobs.

To many whites the exclusion of blacks from the cities seemed the only solution to the problem of violent racial conflict. This sentiment helps explain the strong urban support for the activities of the American Colonization Society, an organization that proposed to ship blacks back to Africa. Other white Northerners preferred to follow the southern practice, which was to remove blacks to the countryside. As one of the more sober observers put it, without some form of total racial separation, "rebellions, amounting to local civil wars, will carry dismay throughout our cities, and drench their streets with blood."[2]

Yet the impulse to expel blacks from the cities was never fully realized. Whites turned instead to another form of social control. By 1860 in most cities above the Mason-Dixon line blacks were "educated in segregated schools, punished in segregated prisons, nursed in segregated hospitals, and buried in segregated cemeteries."[3] By that date, too, segregation of both free and slave blacks was also emerging in southern cities as a supplement to the social discipline of the system of urban slavery, and occupational and housing opportunities became increasingly restricted in both North and South. Regardless of where they lived most free urban blacks seeking work had to accept "nigger jobs," occupations of low pay, low skill, and little responsibility, which

29　Rioters protest the Civil War draft law, which favored the wealthy by permitting exemption for a fee. The scene is the *Tribune* office in New York City, 1863.

30　A home for black orphans is burned and sacked during the Draft Riots in New York City.

frequently involved dirty, dangerous, and extremely arduous tasks. Even the handful of black businessmen in northern cities (who, before the Civil War, catered to whites and earned enough to own their homes) found their economic opportunities and residential choices severely limited by 1880. A close study of Cincinnati's black entrepreneurs in the postbellum generation shows them gradually withdrawing from their former business and dwelling sites in largely white neighborhoods and moving into the poor housing of the poverty-stricken black enclaves.

There is some evidence that blacks in other cities in these years also had to contend with a limited if not reduced range of job choices and strong pressure toward residential segregation. In addition, the continued drive of immigrants for political recognition after the war limited black accomplishments in that sphere and scarred the political process with violence and intimidation above as well as below the Ohio

River. In northern cities, where they seldom constituted more than 5 percent of the population, as in southern centers, where the figures ran much higher, blacks in 1880 held second-class citizenship. The pervasive and tightening systems of segregation and discrimination—both formal and informal—not only stalled the blacks' drive for full participation in civic life, but also threatened to put them in an even more precarious position in the economy and residential structure of the cities. In race relations, as with ethnic and labor disputes, city dwellers continued to rely on violence and intimidation as the court of final resort.

Inadequate Services

Other indices, including the poor performance of city governments, suggest that the cities lurched out of control as the historic walking city dissolved. Though much of the physical plant and many of the municipal institutions characteristic of the twentieth-century city were created between 1840 and 1880, contemporaries constantly complained about inadequate and shabby services and inefficiency and dishonesty on the part of city officials. Nor did the age, location, ethnic mix, or economic structure of particular places make much difference. "The evil," lamented one national magazine in 1870,

> is a general one. We hear more of the defects of city government in New York than elsewhere, because New York is the largest city we have. But . . . Philadelphia and Brooklyn are perhaps quite as corruptly and inadequately governed as New York. New Orleans and Cincinnati rival it clearly. Chicago, by the testimony of its best citizens, was very recently worse governed than any of them.[4]

A variety of factors account for the deplorable performance of city governments in the mid-nineteenth century. One was the aforementioned rapid growth. Municipalities simply found it impossible to keep up with the expanding needs for light, water, sewerage, transportation, education, health facilities, and fire and police protection that accompanied the unexpectedly rapid growth of urban populations and the expanded scale of urban life after 1840. Yet the problems of city government had other sources as well. The question of public health, for

31 A comment on the quality of the public water supply of a Massachusetts community. The large oval teeming with "animalcules" is supposedly a projected drop of local water "magnified by the solar microscope."

example, proved intractable in large part because medical science had not established the causes or remedies for a wide range of infectious diseases. In other instances the inability to forecast accurately the future demand for city services was a cause, for cities grew not only more rapidly than ever in population and area but also in largely unpredictable ways. Time and again technological advances or changes in living

52

styles associated with elevated standards of living rendered service innovations obsolete well before the time anticipated by city officials.

Municipal waterworks, for example, became common in the early nineteenth century and, by 1860, the nation's sixteen largest cities were served by waterworks of some sort, all but four of them municipally owned. But by the same date city officials in some places were facing their second or third water crisis. Boston, with a system designed to deliver 7½ million gallons daily, was one of those places. There, in an effort to control wastage, inspectors patrolled the night streets, listening for the gurgle of running water. Still, water crises persisted and consumption rose. In 1843 it stood at 8½ million gallons, in 1854 it was 14 million, and by 1860 it exceeded 17 million gallons—an average daily consumption of 97 gallons per resident.

In retrospect it seems clear that higher standards of living and technological innovations in plumbing, transportation, and other fields, not wanton wastage, accounted for the soaring usage and the chronic water shortages. The first American patent for the flush toilet was obtained in 1833; a decade later, as many as one-fourth of the houses in the bigger cities contained bathtubs, and after 1850, the use of both these devices spread rapidly. In the same period the increasing concentration of factories in urban settings brought another major water con-

32   Advertizement for the latest innovations in intimate plumbing in 1877.

JENNINGS' SPECIALTIES.

JENNINGS PAT. W. CLOSETS.

IRON TRAP.   ALL E. WARE.

JENNINGS' PATENT LATRINES.

JENNINGS' PATENT TIP-UP WASH BASIN.

JENNINGS' PATENT LATRINES,

Especially adapted for Schools, Railway Stations, etc.

Jennings' Patent Water-Closet,

In one piece Earthenware, with Trap ; also with Iron Trap.

Patent Tip-up Wash-Basins,   Patent Disinfectors,

sumer into the city, and the growing popularity and size of the hotel, another mid-century invention, also contributed to the heavy burden on municipal water supplies. So, too, did the advent of the horse-drawn railway, a mode of rapid transit that not only spurred suburban growth, but increased each city's stock of thirsty horses and mules and contributed to the demand for more effective street flushing. Many suburban towns, like Roxbury, Charleston, Dorchester, Brighton, and West Roxbury in the Boston area, chose annexation to the metropolis rather than undertaking the expensive business of supplying their own water and creating other services. By 1880 American city dwellers ranked among the most prodigious water consumers on the globe, and waterworks commissioners across the country were still inundated with complaints about inadequate service.

Political Chaos

The complex structure of municipal governments also exacerbated the difficulties of providing urban services. By 1840 most American cities modeled their governments on the federal example, including the system of checks and balances, which tended to impede prompt and decisive action by city officials. City councils generally were composed of two houses elected on a ward basis. Mayors, elected at large, had become relatively independent of the legislative branches, and in most places the executive office gradually increased its strength by acquisition of veto power over city ordinances and of wider appointive discretion. But the mayors never accumulated enough power to curb seriously the influence of councilmen determined at all costs to foster the interests of their particular districts. In the absence of a strong central authority, the three branches seldom agreed on priorities and proved chronically unable to raise the taxes necessary to meet the need for new and expanded services.

Recurring financial crises forced city officials to turn to state governments for fiscal assistance. Rural-based state legislators proved niggardly with state tax revenues, but responded with alacrity to these opportunities to broaden their control over the "evil" cities. The confluence of city needs and rural suspicion of urban populations produced a battery of school, park, police, taxation, and other executive boards—some

33 Tallying the vote at a New York City polling place in the presidential election of 1876.

elected and others appointed by state officials or legislatures—and incessant meddling with the structure of city governments through state revision of municipal charters, ostensibly to assure the honest and economical administration of local affairs.

The division and subdivision of powers and the proliferation of offices at the local level confused voters and officeholders alike and contributed greatly to the crisis in urban government. Jersey City had its charter amended by state action 91 times between 1835 and 1875; the New York legislature passed more laws for New York City between 1867 and 1870 than Parliament passed for all the cities of the United Kingdom between 1835 and 1885; and Philadelphia had at one time 30 separate boards to supervise special functions. In 1880, New Haven, Connecticut voters elected a bicameral city council, a sheriff, a mayor, a treasurer, a city clerk, and an auditor; the city's mayor and councilmen selected police, fire, health, and public works commissioners, a board of finance, and several other authorities; and the Connecticut

55

legislature appointed city judges who, in turn, appointed the city attorney. Under these conditions it was virtually impossible for even the best-informed citizen to discover who was responsible for what, and almost as difficult for officials to cope with the municipal maze.

But the roots of the crisis in urban government ran beyond the tangled bureaucracy into the social, economic, political, and demographic dimensions of city life. Part of the problem grew out of the unprecedented size and heterogeneity of the electorate. By 1840, universal male suffrage for white adult citizens was everywhere the rule, and the strong attraction of cities for young men aged 21 to 45 vastly enlarged the numbers eligible for participation in the urban political arena. In addition, the broadening of urban services multiplied the number of available patronage jobs, providing a new incentive for political action among the middle and the lower classes. The ethnic and religious diversity of this enlarged electorate also generated an intense and broad interest in politics. The clash of cultures in the cities raised emotion-laden questions, such as those concerning temperance, Sabbatarianism, the role of religion in the schools, and, after 1865, the place of blacks in urban life—which involved broadening the base of political participation and proved difficult to resolve by compromise.

The advent of the factory and the spread of medium-to-large shops added to the atomization of the urban political system. For the first time numbers of workers labored together in factories rather than in their homes or small, nearby shops, and job competition intensified as their numbers increased. Discontent among those for whom adjustment to this new life was most difficult rose as the more successful skilled workers moved up a notch into the role of coordinator and its accompanying more comfortable life. These new conditions of life and labor generated a pervasive anxiety and uncertainty among the workers. From the first quarter of the nineteenth century into the 1880s, urban politicians in the two major parties had to contend with a series of independent parties that appealed to this dissatisfaction by supporting, among other things, free land, shorter working hours, free public education, and cooperative businesses. Beneath the specific objectives of many of these groups, however, simmered a powerful impulse to retrieve a mythical and neighborly community of love and social and political opportunity, in which every occupation shared an equal status. To these men, as the Knights of Labor expressed it, the "unproductive" —bankers, monopolists, lawyers, and saloonkeepers—constituted the real threat to society.

Working-class unrest was not the only political repercussion of the coming of factory production and the gradual transformation of production routines in older enterprises. The men who financed, managed, and advised the new concerns began to assert their right to a place in political life commensurate with their new economic power and growing social prestige. And as urban areas stretched and their populations grew and diversified, the cities sprouted new neighborhoods, each served by a miscellany of parochial yet ambitious entrepreneurs, including contractors, grocers, butchers, and real estate operators. These "community" spokesmen also had grievances and causes for which they sought political expression, and their numbers and diversity added to the rampant political factionalism.

At the same time two significant groups of citizens who possessed valuable resources in education and money virtually removed themselves from urban politics. This came about as a consequence of the development of the urban-industrial heartland—a highly urbanized strip of territory between New York and Chicago that contained the lion's share of the country's manufacturing capacity—and the emergence of a national economy with an extraordinarily high incidence of commercial contact between cities in the heartland and regional urban centers and subcenters outside the manufacturing core of the continent. As this system took shape, every major city and many of the smaller ones developed a new class of businessman whose chief function was the operation of the complex transportation, communication, financial, and managerial systems upon which the accelerating pace and broadened scope of economic activities depended. These men lost their sense of civic commitment as they moved into interregional and interurban economic affairs.

At the same time, many members of the old mercantile and professional families, their social and political ascendancy challenged by this new class, also turned their backs on the problems of the cities. Some took refuge in utopian communitarian experiments and participated in the establishment of ideal settlements (such as Brook Farm or Oneida), well removed from disorderly cities. But not all descendants of the old urban elite backed away from the challenge of the changing city. Some, including Charles Loring Brace, who dedicated his life to improving urban youth by placing them on farms or in rural towns, Dorothea Dix, who led the way in fighting for the improved treatment of the insane, and Horace Mann, the champion of public education, preached self-help and compassion for the poor and mounted major philanthropic activities. More numerous and equally influential, though less famous, were the city missionaries and middle- and upper-class lay men and

34 The Ladies' Home Mission provides dinner for the children of the poor on Thanksgiving Day, 1858.

women in cities across the country who established hospitals, societies for the prevention of pauperism, and a vast array of other relief and moral reform agencies at the local level. In the process, these various leaders helped alert the nation to the prevalence of poverty and to the need for a commitment among the elite to help the urban poor.

In the disorganized and divided urban society politics fell into disarray. Most places no longer possessed generally acknowledged "natural leaders," who could spend their leisure serving the city through government and who could, by virtue of their prestige, command enough support to exert a stabilizing influence. As the authority of ruling elites declined, politics became virtually a full-time occupation that, for the first time, required its practitioners to organize masses of voters whose beliefs, concerns, backgrounds, needs, and aspirations varied incredibly. But even "professional" politicians found it impossible to organize the heterogeneous and factionalized urban electorate into a continuing majority behind a viable political program. Some voters were captivated by the opportunities and adventure of mobility—socioeconomic or physical; others were distracted by first one and then another reform movement; and, in still others, constructive political participation was ruled out by confusion and indifference or by ethnic, religious, or racial prejudice.

Unable to create broad-based and effective coalitions, politicians accomplished what they could by using patronage, special favors, and bribery to persuade individuals and groups to cooperate on specific projects. More than any other factor, this mode of resolving the crisis of political leadership accounted for the astonishingly high cost of municipal improvements and services in the mid-nineteenth century. In the decade between 1865 and 1875, the population of the country's fifteen major cities rose by 70 percent, but their debt rose 271 percent. Costs of projects always exceeded estimates, and while the additional expense seldom was more than two or three times the original projection, one New York City courthouse originally budgeted for a quarter of a million dollars ultimately cost 14 million dollars.

Few contemporary observers, however, attributed municipal financial chaos or governmental ineptitude to the disrupted state of society produced by the process of urbanization after 1840. They preferred, in-

35 One of two cartoons entitled "Two Great Questions" by political cartoonist Thomas Nast in 1871. The question in this case: "Who stole the people's money?" The answer: "'Twas him."

stead, to pin the blame on infamous "bosses" like William Marcy Tweed of New York or Alexander Shepherd of Washington, D.C. Though urban historians have not yet agreed on who governed the mid-nineteenth-century cities, the evidence suggests that it was not the bosses. With occasional exceptions, notably James McManes of Philadelphia, most mid-century bosses dominated the politics of their cities for periods of less than five years, and more often than not they exercised only a tenuous control over their followers, a fact that helps explain the extraordinarily high level and pervasiveness of corruption. In the final analysis it was the low level of political tolerance, the unwillingness or inability to build give-and-take alliances into cohesive and enduring ruling coalitions, not bossism, that produced the inept urban governments of the mid-nineteenth century. Too many city dwellers held the values and goals of their fellow citizens in deep contempt for any politician to mold the complex and shifting elements of city life into a machine. On this score, Tweed, the most notorious boss of the era, was neither better nor worse than others. "This population," he contended after his downfall, "is too hopelessly split up into races and factions to govern it under universal suffrage, except by the bribery of patronage or corruption."[5]

Tweed's assessment of the sources of the divisiveness that tore the urban political fabric was on the mark, but his formula for resolving the conflicts proved short-sighted and inadequate. Tweed's short career as boss demonstrates that even the most callous practitioner of patronage and corruption could not govern for long. In this view neither bosses nor their critics commanded the knowledge, skills, technology, or power to harness the complex and divisive forces that created the mid-nineteenth-century urban crisis. The magnitude of the first urban explosion made the cities virtually ungovernable, and reasonably effective and efficient systems of urban politics developed only after 1880, with the completion of changes that transformed the city and set the stage for two generations of urban creativity.

Notes

[1] Quoted in Richard C. Wade, "The City in History—Some American Perspectives," in Werner Z. Hirsch, ed., *Urban Life and Form* (New York: Holt, 1963), p. 62.

[2] Henry D. Shapiro and Zane L. Miller, eds., *Physician to the West: The Writings of Daniel Drake on Science and Society* (Lexington: The Univ. Press of Kentucky, 1970), p. xxxiv.

[3] Leon Litwack, *North of Slavery: The Negro in the Free States, 1790–1860* (Chicago: The Univ. of Chicago Press, 1961), p. 97.

[4] *Hunt's Merchants Magazine and Commerical Review*, LXIII (Dec., 1870), 433-34.

[5] Quoted in Charles N. Glaab and A. Theodore Brown, *A History of Urban America* (New York: Macmillan, 1967), p. 205.

Bibliography

Belcher, Wyatt W. *The Economic Rivalry Between St. Louis and Chicago, 1850–1880.* New York: Columbia Univ. Press, 1947. An exhaustive treatment of one of the most important mid-nineteenth-century urban imperialist clashes.

Blake, Nelson M. *Water for the Cities: A History of the Urban Water Supply Problem in the United States.* Syracuse, N.Y.: Syracuse Univ. Press, 1956. One of the lamentably few monographs devoted to the development of basic municipal services. The emphasis is on New York, Philadelphia, and Boston in the nineteenth century.

Chandler, Alfred D. J. "The Beginnings of 'Big Business' in American Industry," *Business History Review,* XXXIII (Spring, 1959), 1–31. An excellent study of business innovations and urbanization. Though it focuses on the last two decades of the nineteenth century, it also reaches back into the middle years of the century.

Ernst, Robert. *Immigrant Life in New York City, 1825–1863.* New York: King's Crown Press, 1949. Discusses German and Irish immigrants and provides additional evidence that newcomers tended to concentrate in peripheral wards. It contains powerful descriptions of housing conditions.

Handlin, Oscar. *Boston's Immigrants: A Study in Acculturation.* Cambridge, Mass.: Harvard Univ. Press, 1956. Deals best with the Irish, but covers only the period to 1865. Boston receives as much attention as the immigrants.

Hofstadter, Richard. *The Age of Reform: From Bryan to F. D. R.* New York: Knopf, 1955. Centered on the Populist-Progressive era, but contains an excellent account of nineteenth-century agriculture, which stresses the peculiar nature of American rural culture and contains a provocative analysis of urban-rural relationship.

Holt, Michael F. *Forging a Majority: The Formation of the Republican Party in Pittsburgh, 1848–1860.* New Haven, Conn.: Yale Univ. Press, 1969. The best study of mid-nineteenth-century urban politics. It traces the breakdown of the democratic process in one city and, by implication, suggests that another revision concerning the causes of the Civil War may be in order.

Knights, Peter R. *The Plain People of Boston, 1830–1860: A Study in City Growth.* New York: Oxford Univ. Press, 1971. An impressive and readable "quantitative history" of geographic and socioeconomic mobility in a mid-nineteenth-century city.

Niehaus, Earl F. *The Irish in New Orleans, 1800–1860.* Baton Rouge, La.: State Univ. Press, 1965. Contains findings that dovetail nicely with those of Handlin on Boston. Underscores the disordered state of mid-nineteenth-century cities.

Reed, Merle E. *New Orleans and the Railroads: The Struggle for Commercial Empire, 1830–1860.* Baton Rouge, La.: State Univ. Press, 1966. A good case study of the difficulties river cities faced in adjusting to the advent of the railroad.

Reinders, Robert C. *End of an Era: New Orleans, 1850–1860.* New Orleans: Pelican Publishing Company, 1964. Complements Holt's work on Pittsburgh and suggests that southern cities did not escape the social and political turmoil that all but paralyzed the democratic process in northern places.

Thernstrom, Stephan. *Poverty and Progress: Social Mobility in a Nineteenth Century City.* Cambridge, Mass.: M.I.T. Press and Harvard Univ. Press, 1964. Illustrates the importance of home ownership and offers a critical evaluation of the "rags to riches" myth.

Wade, Richard C. *Slavery in the Cities: The South, 1820–1860.* New York: Oxford Univ. Press, 1964. Lays out the peculiar nature of the mid-nineteenth-century urban crisis in the South. Its significance for understanding nineteenth-century cities extends well beyond that indicated by the title.

Ward, David. *Cities and Immigrants: A Geography of Change in Nineteenth Century America.* New York: Oxford Univ. Press, 1971. Broader in focus than the title suggests, it covers the period 1790–1920 and analyzes physical mobility, social geography, and land use patterns of cities as well as urbanization in a regional economic framework.

The Emergence of 3
Metropolitan America

The mid-nineteenth-century urban crisis was never resolved. It gave way, instead, to another and equally perplexing one stemming from profound changes in the demographic, economic, and geographic structure of the nation's urban centers. Between 1880 and 1910, American cities and the national economic and political structures assumed the shape they would retain for nearly fifty years. Throughout the period, rural-urban migration and foreign immigration persisted, and the proportion of the nation's total population that ranked as urban continued to rise. Equally important, technological innovations in mass rapid transit provided the means by which the gradual mid-nineteenth-century expansion of the territorial limits of cities gave way to urban sprawl. These developments established the environment in which the nation's economic structure shifted from a commercial to an industrial orientation. The rapid physical and population growth of cities created vast new markets for manufactured goods, and the entrepreneurial response to these demands carried the economy from the mixed commercial, manufacturing, and agrarian phase characterized by diversity in the scale and managerial structure of business organizations into the industrial phase dominated by large, mass-production corporations.

Urbanization after 1880 also laid the groundwork for important political changes. The steady increase in the proportion of people living in cities enhanced the urban influence in politics, contributed to the declining status and prestige of rural life, and sparked a farmers' revolt that centered its rhetoric on cities and elements of American life commonly associated with cities. At the same time the spatial expansion of urban areas sparked a reshuffling of the interior social and economic geography of cities. Forced to adjust simultaneously to a novel urban structure and a new corporate-industrial economy, city dwellers after 1880 tended to vote for the party that seemed most willing to meet major issues with an active, positive exercise of federal power. While we now think of the Democratic Party as the party of the big cities and as the advocate of vigorous central government, it was the Republican organization that benefited most from the fundamental alteration of the rural-urban balance and the anxieties of city voters seeking to adjust to a new urban and industrial society. Capitalizing on its mid-nineteenth-century image as the party of forceful government, the GOP built a national majority based on its strong support among urban voters. The end of the nineteenth century brought not only a new kind of city and a new national economic structure, but also a new urban-centered system of national politics dominated by the Republican Party.

THE SHIFT TO AN URBAN-INDUSTRIAL BASE

The magnitude of both the physical and population aspects of urban growth was impressive. While horse-drawn street railways were already producing cities of unprecedented geographic dimensions by the 1880s, the introduction and rapid spread of cable-powered cars and electric trolleys after that date accelerated the rate of decentralization. By 1900 the walking city, covering five to eight square miles, had been replaced

36 Brooklyn Bridge in 1898, when it carried an "el" train and a streetcar line. View is from Brooklyn, which became part of New York City in the same year.

by distended metropolises spreading over twenty, fifty, and more square miles. In 1880, 28.2 percent of the American people lived in cities. A decade later the figure stood at 35.1, at the turn of the century it reached 39.7, and in 1910 it rose to 45.7 percent. In absolute figures, 44,639,989 people lived in cities in 1910, up from a mark of 6,216,518 fifty years earlier.

The geographic expansion of cities and the consequent extension of services into the newly settled edges created a sudden and spiraling demand for producers' goods. The expansion of lighting, heating, power, transportation, water, sewerage, telegraph, and telephone facilities in the new cities absorbed ever growing quantities of electric lighting apparatus, copper wire, streetcars, iron, steel, and lead pipe. In addition, the rising volume of residential, office, and factory construction in and about cities created enlarged markets for power, construction machinery, and explosives as well as for metals, and the continued rapid increase of the urban population established vast outlets for a host of new consumer goods, including the sewing machine, typewriter, bicycle, and, eventually, the automobile. Firms manufacturing these goods provided yet another avenue of growth for the "heavy" or "basic" producers' goods industries.

The impact of these new demands for both producers' and consumers' goods completed the shift in the economy from a city-organized agricultural and commercial base to an urban-industrial base. As late as 1870 the major manufacturers, except those that serviced the expanding railway system, processed agricultural goods and provided farmers with food and clothing. Forty years later, however, many more major firms made producers' goods ticketed for use by industries rather than by rural or urban consumers. In 1909, for example, 36 of the nation's 50 largest manufacturers were making producers' goods, and the list included such currently familiar names as United States Steel, General Electric, and Westinghouse. By the opening of the twentieth century, in short, American society had become industrial, and the growing cities had provided the markets that stimulated this critical expansion in the manufacturing sector of the economy.

Effects on the Business Economy

The challenge of filling the immense urban demand for manufactured goods produced several important innovations in the business economy. The most important business leaders of the new era were neither masters of finance nor of invention and technological development. Instead, men like Rockefeller, Carnegie, Procter and Gamble, and the DuPonts made their distinctive contributions in the fields of management and marketing. This first generation of American organization men put together a new kind of business organization of unequaled size, complexity, and productive capacity. This institution, the vertically integrated corporation, combined the major economic processes—the acquisition of raw materials, manufacturing, packaging, marketing, and finance—into one centralized bureaucracy, whose chief operating principle was efficiency. Though relatively few in number, the vastly powerful new corporations had a dominant influence in the economy.

Advertizing   These giant enterprises also altered the climate of business competition in a manner that paved the way for the appearance of a new kind of advertizing. As the competition in any one line of goods narrowed to a contest among a few very large corporations, management decision-makers concentrated more on developing and maintaining a share of the total market than on undertaking futile and destructive campaigns to drive their competitors to the wall by underselling, buying out, or absorbing other companies. But this live and let live "oligopolistic" situation did not mean that big corporations existed in a wholly secure environment. In order to maintain a share of the market commensurate with the immense productive capacities of the new firms, corporate managers felt compelled to encourage demand for their products among consumers. As a result, annual national expenditures for advertizing skyrocketed from $27 million in 1880 to $95 million in 1900.

Much of this increase came from money spent on campaigns to condition consumers to prefer the advertized brand. In the 1880s several soap firms, including Procter & Gamble, the makers of Ivory soap, pioneered in this practice, which spread rapidly thereafter; by 1905, *Printer's Ink* heralded the twentieth century as the "golden age" of trade brand advertizing. It was now possible, the editor asserted, for a manufacturer to clear the market of "dozens of mongrel, unknown, unacknowledged makes of a fabric, a dress-essential, [or] a food" by adopting a standard trade brand and backing it with national advertizing that would "lay down the lines of a demand that will not only grow with the years . . . but will become, in some degree, a monopoly."[1]

But the new advertizing went beyond product differentiation in seeking to control the consumer market. Another objective was to create consumer demand where there had not been any. In 1903, Walter Dill Scott, a staunch advocate of this approach, urged the demand stimulation technique on the producers' community. How many businessmen, he asked in an article on the psychology of advertizing, "describe the piano so vividly that the reader can hear it: How many food products are so described that the reader can taste the food? . . . How many describe an undergarment so that the reader can feel the pleasant contact with his body?"[2] Several, of course, had already adopted this tactic, includ-

37 An early advertizement for Ivory soap, so decorous that the product name appears only in the text.

ing P & G, which, by touting Ivory soap as "ninety-nine and forty-four one-hundredths percent pure," suggested that city consumers needed lots of Ivory to protect them from dirt, smoke, infection, and, by implication, uncleanliness of other sorts.

REGIONAL STABILITY

Despite these sharp changes in the organization, competitive milieu, and marketing strategy within the business economy, the emergence of an industrial corporate society had surprisingly little effect on the relationship among the nation's economic regions or on regional differentials in rates of urbanization. Although the big businesses sold their goods in a national market, the jobs created by the increased productive capacity of the producers' and consumers' goods industries were not spread evenly among cities in every region of the country. They concentrated, instead, in the urban-industrial heartland, where the corporations had ready access to raw materials and large pools of skilled and semiskilled workers and managerial talent. To be sure, between 1870 and 1910 the proportion of the labor force employed in manufacturing rose for every region in the nation, and the gap between the heartland and the other regions in this respect tended to narrow. Nonetheless, in 1910, the New England, Middle Atlantic, and Great Lakes states reported respectively 49.1, 39.8, and 33.2 percent of their labor force in manufacturing, while the other regions all fell below the national average of 27.9 percent. Since industry ranked as the chief stimulant of regional prosperity and economic influence, the manufacturing belt not only retained but strengthened its mid-nineteenth-century position of economic dominance.

The Northeast

The uneven regional distribution of employment in manufacturing and the preference of industrialists for urban sites also account for the persistence of mid-nineteenth-century patterns of regionally differentiated levels of urbanization. In 1910, as a half century before, the Northeast, with 70 percent of the nation's total urban population, remained the most heavily urbanized region, and no other section could match its mix of great, large, and intermediate-sized urban areas. In 1910, 64 percent of the Northeast's population lived in cities, and the region contained 34 of the country's 50 cities with populations over 100,000 as well as 14 of the 19 cities with over 250,000 inhabitants. In addition, most of the nation's intermediate-sized places clustered in the heartland. Of the country's total of 49 cities with populations between 50,000 and 100,000 in 1910, 42 fell within the boundaries of the manufacturing belt.

38   Factory scene about 1910.

The West and South

Although city growth in the regions beyond the industrial heartland continued in these years, the pattern of urbanization in the outlying areas differed from that of the Northeast. Outside the manufacturing belt the proportion of urban residents in the total regional population remained lower, with the biggest places seldom exceeding 500,000 residents, and fewer intermediate-sized places—50,000 to 75,000 people—developing. Nonetheless, by 1910 the centers that would dominate the West, the Southwest, and the South into the mid-twentieth century had emerged.

The completion of the transcontinental railroads and of branch feeders to these trunk lines spurred city growth in the interior and Far West and produced challengers to the commercial dominance that San Francisco and St. Louis had exercised over this entire area in the mid-nineteenth century. Population figures reflected the changing configuration. In 1910, San Francisco still led the Far West, but the census takers counted 250,000 people in Los Angeles and over 200,000 in both Seattle and Portland. The rapid growth of these and other places helped push the urban proportion of the total population in the Far West to 56 per-

39 Downtown Seattle in 1904, when the city was nearing the 200,000 mark in population.

cent, a figure that gave that region a level of urbanization second only to that of the manufacturing belt. By 1910, too, the pattern of important centers in the interior West had developed. Minneapolis-St. Paul, with over 500,000 inhabitants, Kansas City and Denver, with more than 200,000, and Omaha with over 100,000, had by that date not only eclipsed the other mid-nineteenth-century competitors for regional dominance, but had also broken the hold of St. Louis and San Francisco on the supply and marketing activities in the Plains States.

Although cities continued to grow in the Southwest and Dixie after 1880, the pace and level of urbanization there lagged well behind that of the other regions. In the Southwest only 22 percent of the population placed in the urban rubric in 1910, and although Dallas, Houston, and San Antonio had entered periods of rapid growth, none had established a clear commercial primacy in this period. The South urbanized at an even slower rate. In 1910 only 20 percent of its total population lived in cities. The biggest cities, New Orleans and Louisville, owed their pre-eminence to their traditional commercial ties with the Old Northwest, not to the internal economic development of the South, and in 1910 both cities ranked lower in the national population hierarchy than in 1870. Nashville, Memphis, and Richmond, with populations between 110,000 and 131,000, retained their leading positions within their immediate areas, but Atlanta and Birmingham were growing more rapidly. Nonetheless, Atlanta's dominance over the Southeast in 1910 supported but 154,000 people, and iron and steel manufacture in Birmingham only 132,000.

POPULATION

Despite regional variations in the pace of urban growth, the fact remains that the population of cities everywhere pushed upward in these years. For the first time, moreover, a significant proportion of the new city dwellers came from natural increase. As a result of improvements in urban sanitation and public health, birth rates rose and death rates dropped in the cities. While statistics on these are scarce and not entirely dependable, it seems clear that in these years the cities abandoned their traditional role as consumers of people. Although the unreliability of the data precludes a precise statement about the dimensions of urban

71

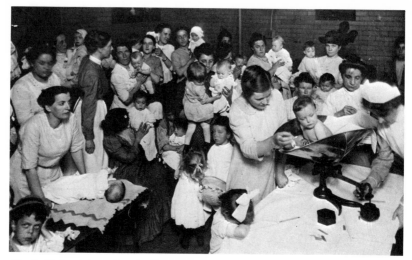

40 A clinic of the Infant Welfare Society in Chicago about 1911, when the urban birth rate was moving sharply upward.

population growth attributable to natural increase, one student of the subject has suggested that between 1860 and 1920 roughly 35 percent of the new city dwellers derived from the increase of births over deaths within the urban environment.

Rural-to-Urban Flow

Throughout the period from 1880 to 1910, however, most of the new urban population came not from natural increase, but from the internal and international movement of people. The rural-to-urban flow within the United States after 1880, as in the mid-nineteenth century, stemmed from the combined influence of push and pull factors. Though the rural population did not decline in absolute terms, the continued improvement of agricultural techniques reduced the demand for farm laborers to such an extent that the high fertility and low death rates in uncongested rural areas produced an "excess" farm population, which was attracted to the cities by the economic opportunities created by the growth of mass production industries.

This push-pull mechanism produced especially dramatic population shifts during the last two decades of the nineteenth century. In the 1880s, for example, 40 percent of the rural townships declined in population. The drain was most severe in the manufacturing belt. In New England, 60 percent of the townships recorded a population loss, over half the townships in Ohio and Illinois suffered in the same way, and Michigan counted 7500 fewer farmers in 1890 than ten years before. But the rural-to-urban push was general, and it persisted into the twentieth century. In 1910, about 11 million, or roughly 20 percent of the nation's total of 45 million city dwellers, had formerly lived on American farms.

To many migrating farmers the future clearly lay with the city, and many evidently agreed with the judgment of the novelist who labeled the nineteenth century a "century of cities." Cities, he noted, "have given their own twist to the progress of the age—and the farmer is as far out of it as if he lived in Alaska. Perhaps there was a time when a man could live in what the poet calls daily communication with nature and not starve his mind or dwarf his soul, but this isn't the century."[3]

Immigration

Immigrants were also engaged in a quest for broader opportunities, and they made up another important component of the new urban population. In the two generations after 1880 the decennial census counted more new arrivals per decade than ever. Between 1900 and 1909 alone some 8.2 million people landed on American shores, and the total for the forty-year span from 1880 to 1920, when the great era of foreign immigration closed, came to almost 23.5 million, while the average number of arrivals per decade amounted to about 6 million individuals. The bulk of the newcomers settled in cities. In 1920, three-quarters of the foreign-born white population lived in cities, 48 percent of the nation's total urban population came from abroad or descended from foreign parentage, and in cities of over 100,000, the foreign-born and their children comprised 58 percent of the population.

Sources In the same period the principal source of immigrants shifted from northern to southern and eastern Europe. Before 1880 some 85 percent of all immigrants came from the British Isles, Germany, British America, and Scandanavia. But by the turn of the century, newcomers from Italy and the Russian and Austro-Hungarian Empires accounted for half the total immigration. From that point on emigration from the old sources declined, and during the decade of the First World War immigrants from northern Europe represented only 20 percent of the total.

A variety of factors account for this shift in the geographic origins of immigrants. The improvement of economic conditions within Germany and Sweden and the increasing attraction of Australia and Canada to emigrants from the British Isles reduced the flow of "old" immigrants. The influx from new sources grew out of the political persecution of Jews in Russia, the removal of restraints on emigration from Slavic areas of the Austro-Hungarian Empire, and the strong desire of many in all these areas to avoid enforced conscription. But changing labor needs within the American economy and the relatively slow pace of economic development in eastern and southern Europe also played a role. The peasants and small townsmen of southern and eastern Europe viewed the abundant unskilled and semiskilled jobs as day laborers or factory workers in the new economy of the United States as far more attractive opportunities than did residents of the more economically advanced countries of northern Europe. And the close synchronization of the number of immigrant arrivals with the flux of the American business cycle after 1870 suggests that the labor demands of the American economy strongly influenced the volume of immigration.

Patterns of Settlement   Most of the so-called "new" immigrants settled in the urban-industrial heartland, though they did not distribute themselves evenly among the cities of the area. Italians and Russians tended to concentrate in the eastern half of the heartland in centers that offered highly diversified job opportunities. A larger proportion of those from the Hapsburg Empire, however, moved inland from the cities of the Mid-Atlantic states. Immigrants from Hapsburg territories that later became Austria and Czechoslovakia gravitated toward the urban centers of the North Central states, but those from what later became Poland, Hungary, and Yugoslavia (and who constituted the majority of emigrants from those areas) settled almost exclusively in the East North Central cities that specialized in heavy industry, though many made their homes in New York, Cleveland, Detroit, Chicago, and Mil-

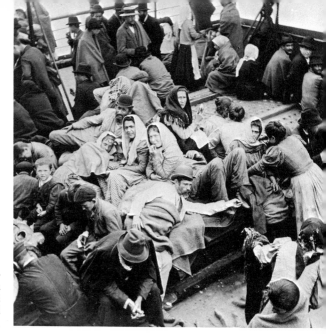

41 One source of the turn-of-the-century increase in urban population: immigrants, seen on the steerage deck of a vessel making the crossing about 1890.

waukee. Cities on the edge of the heartland, such as Baltimore, Cincinnati, and St. Louis, and places beyond the core attracted smaller proportions of southern and eastern Europeans, although New Orleans developed a vital Italian community, and several West Coast cities, especially San Francisco and Los Angeles, housed significant numbers of Chinese and smaller enclaves of Japanese.

CITY STRUCTURE

Whatever the composition of its population, the post-1880 city possessed a distinctive interior structure. After 1880, the above-mentioned improvement in transport and communications technologies, as well as a spate of construction innovations, such as the elevator, accelerated the mid-nineteenth century expansion and the development of central business districts. This also instituted a sorting-out process that created a more intensely specialized system of land use and residential segregation. The consequences were ironic. As the acreage of cities doubled, tripled, and quadrupled, part of the population and certain kinds of economic activities concentrated near the centers of the metropolises, while other people, industries, and businesses scattered toward the periphery. The play of these centripetal and centrifugal influences

42 Fountain Square (about 1905), heart of Cincinnati's central business district in the early twentieth century.

made urban sprawl, a higher skyline, central-city commercial and traffic congestion, and a constant shifting of residential neighborhoods and economic districts the hallmarks of the late-nineteenth- and early-twentieth-century city.

Downtown and the Central Business District

While downtown in the mid-nineteenth-century walking city had been dominated by warehouses, small workshops, and embryo financial districts, the technological changes at the turn of the century and the increased purchasing power of a large segment of the urban population rearranged land use patterns and concentrated a wide range of economic activities at the core of the new cities. Some deplored the change; others applauded. One old resident of Cincinnati complained in 1904 that Third Street, once the "Wall Street" of his town, now looked abandoned, "squalid and dismal . . . , grimy and greasy." But a year later a local paper crowed that in the preceding twelve months real estate men had invested $3 million for new buildings, alterations, and renovations

76

within a ten-block area centered on Fountain Square, the heart of the Queen City's new central business district.

By 1910, Cincinnati and every other major town sported an incredibly congested central business district easily identified by a bulging wedge of skyscrapers towering above the surrounding mass of three-, four-, and five-story buildings. Within and on the fringes of this region specialization of land use was most intense. Banks, department stores, wholesalers, and physicians and lawyers tended to cluster, and club, theater, restaurant, hotel, and low-brow entertainment districts emerged, each possessing a commonly known though shifting and seldom precisely defined set of boundaries.

Shopping comprised the chief new function of downtown. Before 1870, most general retailing had been unspecialized and widely dispersed throughout the city. After that date, however, the increasing size of the local market and the heightened accessibility of central locations encouraged more wholesalers and new entrepreneurs to establish separate retail establishments in the heart of the city. The organization of department stores, which, because of the large scale of their operations, could offer a variety of goods at low prices, completed the creation of a separate and extensive centrally located retail district. The big new emporiums hovered around focal points in the street railway system, while specialty and luxury goods outlets sought locations near hotels, financial districts, and high-income areas where they could most conveniently reach their wealthy clientele. But both these retailers and the department stores derived much of their business from the growing numbers of commuters who came daily to the central business district to work.

Despite the diversification of economic activities and the appearance of large retail districts in the core, several important industries clung to their central locations. Most were small enterprises or branches of manufacturing that adhered to the mid-nineteenth-century practice of performing the various steps in the production process in separate places within a relatively narrow geographic radius. Printing and publishing industries, for example, expanded by the proliferation of small-scale operations within or adjacent to downtown. The clothing industry retained its central location because the merchant-manufacturers who dominated the business still relied on a series of shops to complete the sequence of production of given items. Yet rising costs caused by inefficiencies associated with traffic congestion and the competition for space tended to reduce the attraction of central locations for even these manufacturers. For years they sought to unclog the streets and reduce the pressure for business sites downtown by agitating for the construction of elevated street railways and subways and the consolidation of scattered railroad terminals. When these improvements failed to clear the streets and thin commercial activities in central business districts, the downtown manufacturers turned to the regulation of land use through zoning to preserve their traditional sites and production procedures.

The larger consumers' and producers' goods manufacturers either moved to or selected new sites away from the downtown districts. Generally, they strung out along major intercity transportation routes. As early as the 1880s, for example, Procter & Gamble in Cincinnati and the Pullman Car Company in Chicago constructed plants next to railroad lines well removed from the central business district. The continued improvement of intraurban transportation and communications facilities accelerated this trend, and by the turn of the century most

43   Traffic in downtown Chicago in 1910.

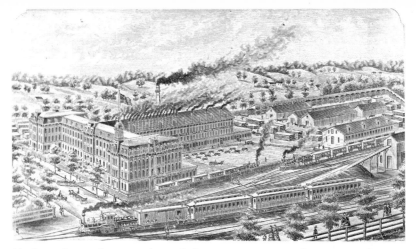

44 Late-nineteenth-century heavy industry at some remove from major urban centers: the Studebaker plant (wagons) at South Bend, Indiana, about fifty miles from Chicago.

major centers possessed several industrial concentrations lying at irregular intervals from the commercial core. Some manufacturers, however, chose locations even farther out, and the settlement of workers nearby created "satellite cities," such as Gary, Indiana. But the outward spread of the population from the major centers ultimately filled the intervening spaces between the metropolis and satellite with residential and neighborhood retail developments.

Residential Patterns

The new city also displayed a distinctive residential structure, one which precisely reversed the social geography of the walking city. Although the pattern in detail varied from place to place, the residential configuration of major cities divided generally into three broad sections, based primarily on income. The new modes of intracity transportation, especially the electric trolley and, after 1910, the automobile, cab, and bus, played a critical role in producing this tripartite division. The improved speed and power of these new transportation facilities snapped the bonds of convenience that had held the wealthy to sites near the focus of their social, economic, and political activities in the center of town. Some complained about a favored old neighborhood that had gone "to ruin almost as if a bombshell had sent it to destruction" or a familiar plaza now become the "loafing place for the most disreputable and worthless vagabonds of both sexes." But whether repelled by the decline of residential districts near downtown or lured by the new accessibility of suburban life, members of the elite now pushed out to settlements of very low density on the periphery of the city.

Electric rapid transit also provided middle-income groups with increased residential latitude, and they, like the rich, pushed away from the center. Since the middle classes could not afford the high cost of housing and living on the urban fringe, they stopped short of the periphery and occupied a broad and more densely built up new district. In most cities these neighborhoods lay beyond what had been the area of lower-class peripheral residence in the walking city of the 1840s and 1850s. Though not as spacious as suburbs, in these middle-class districts men could, as one of them observed, "rear their families out where the sun shines, out where at least a fair portion of pure air and sunlight will be theirs."[4]

The poor in the new city lacked the freedom of residential choice of the other two groups. Consequently, the lower classes were left behind in districts that in the mid-nineteenth century had been slums. As the city's total population rose and shifted outward, the poor moved into the abandoned houses of the wealthy and former dwelling sites of the middle-income groups near the expanding central business district. In the late nineteenth century these shifts of population distribution produced the familiar pattern of the modern metropolis. The rich claimed the periphery, the poor and the newcomers the "inner" city, and the middle classes the region between the slums and suburbs.

Differing levels of income was not the only factor that set these districts apart as distinctive sections of the city. The slums, for example, topped the other two areas in disease, death, crime, and illiteracy rates, and placed last in the statistics on home ownership. Housing in the inner city was also more diverse than elsewhere. Slum dwellers lived in shanties, cellars, tenements, converted warehouses and factories, as well as in the once fashionable homes that had now been subdivided into small rental units. Conditions in all these places appalled outsiders, and reformers in every city compiled long lists of inner-city housing "evils," including "dark halls, damp, ill-ventilated, gloomy rooms, [a] lack of adequate water supply, . . . drainage, privies, catchbasins

80

45 and 46 New York's East Side
about 1900: at right, a tenement
bedroom; below, one of the streets
of the area.

and outdoor toilets," and grievously overcrowded dwellings containing "twenty-eight families, another . . . from forty to fifty families, another . . . thirteen families."[5]

Ethnic and Religious Patterns

The ethnic and religious affiliations of slum residents were even more heterogeneous than their housing accommodations, especially in the cities in the industrial heartland. Yet the low-income districts of virtually every big city contained at least some "new" as well as "old" immigrants, a smaller contingent of native white migrants from rural districts, and, depending on whether the city lay above or below the Mason-Dixon line, varying proportions of blacks. Only the blacks, however, appeared in highly segregated enclaves, for the other groups seldom gathered in homogeneous concentrations above 60 percent in any given neighborhood, block, street, or building.

In the slums religious diversity also reached a peak. Catholic parishes reflected ethnic origins. Jews worshiped in synagogues often distinguished by differences in the cultural origins of their worshipers as well as by the broader division between the Orthodox and Conservative branches of Judaism. Protestants differed in a number of ways—by race, denomination, ethnic affiliation, and individual religious predisposition as in the case of self-proclaimed preachers who held services in abandoned storefronts.

Unlike those in the outer residential regions, slum dwellers were still chiefly concerned with the struggle for survival. They pursued a bewildering variety of occupations, including unskilled labor (the principal employment), various small-business jobs, and the professions. Many of the newcomers, harried by the confused babble about them and hounded by the high incidence of death, disease, vice, crime, and unemployment, proved unable to scratch out an existence above the subsistence level. Yet others, perhaps most, managed either to improve their lot, hold their own, or boost their children up and out. But poverty, transiency, and unfamiliarity with urban life and American society made it almost impossible for slum dwellers to create a lasting network of voluntary associations that could effectively shield them from economic and social distress and teach them valuable organizational skills. And always there were more new arrivals to fill the vacancies and perpetuate the process of adjustment in the neighborhood.

Zone of Emergence

Distance outward from the slums correlated not only with improvement of living conditions but with a narrowing of the range of housing, occupational, ethnic, and religious diversity. In the lower-middle- and middle-income neighborhoods those living closest to the slums rented tenement apartments, but farther out, double- and triple-deckers and single-family cottages, complete with trees and a patch of grass, were more common. More families there owned or were in the process of purchasing their homes, a larger proportion of children attended school, and the incidence of disease, death, and crime ran below the appallingly high levels of the inner city. Although the region contained groups representative of the city's entire spectrum of occupational, religious, and ethnic elements, skilled laborers and better-paid factory workers, Irish and German Catholics, evangelical Protestants, and second-generation urbanites—usually of "old" immigrant stock—tended to predominate. Though some residents of these neighborhoods walked to work in near-

47   About 1900, new homes in an outlying residential district—Gary, Indiana, just outside of Chicago.

by factories, shops, or offices, significant numbers commuted to jobs in crowded streetcars on which "people suffocate, struggle in the crush, and are finally landed somewhere—for five cents."

Dubbed the "Zone of Emergence" by social workers, this region housed a population that had made a relatively successful adjustment to the economic routine of the new city and had moved well along the road to assimilation into American urban culture. Yet its inhabitants enjoyed but marginal economic security, for strikes, layoffs, industrial accidents, depressions, and the absence of old-age and other welfare programs clouded their lives with the fear of poverty. Their halfway position in the process of assimilation intensified their sense of insecurity, as did their residence on or near the cutting edge of the expanding slums. All the talk among capitalists "about 'splendid ambitions and aspirations,'" wrote one embittered German-speaking resident of the Zone, "is for the fortunate few; but we want them for the many."[6]

Threatened by poverty and absorption into the expanding slums, Zone residents assumed a defensive posture that expressed itself in a passion for organizational affiliation. This section of the city, as one reporter put it, housed the "so-called middle class . . . ," a class in which "there are many organizations, societies, associations, fraternities and clubs that bring together people who are striving upward, trying to uplift themselves."[7] Many belonged to building associations, savings institutions that catered especially to those of modest means who aspired to home ownership. Unions also garnered most of their members from among the residents of the Zone, but singing societies, rifle clubs, bowling leagues, mutual-benefit associations, charity organizations, and groups devoted to educational uplift also flourished in this region. So, too, did ethnic associations, almost all of which offered their members economic assistance while at the same time seeking to protect Old World customs against the erosion of assimilation and the tendency of the second and third generations to plunge headlong into American ways. The conflicts of loyalties and the economic vulnerability and social insecurity, which motivated the joiner spirit in this area, made the Zone the most politically unpredictable section of the city, and, in times of economic stress, social tension, or industrial conflict, many of its inhabitants were easy prey for religious and racial bigots.

The Suburban Fringe

Beyond the Zone, on the "cool green rim of the city," leading business and influential families occupied the wealthiest, safest, healthiest, and least diverse residential neighborhoods in the new city. The general affluence of the upper classes gave them access to the best that turn-of-the-century urban centers offered in housing, education, medical care, and physical environment, and here the statistical indicators of distress ran strikingly lower than in either of the other two districts. Yet the aura of stability veiled a certain uneasiness, for even the silk-stocking neighborhoods were not wholly exempt from the insecurity and sense of impermanence that troubled others in the new city. Thieves from the inner wards found rich pickings among the mansions of the wealthy on the periphery, and the sudden death or crippling of a relative or close friend by one or another of the yet unconquered contagious illnesses underscored the "poverty of riches" in confrontations with diseases rooted in the unsanitary conditions of the inner city. The bulk of the fringe population, moreover, was comprised of pioneers uprooted from the older, once fashionable areas nearer downtown, and that experience with the forces of change sensitized them to residential and other land use shifts that might endanger their new neighborhoods. This suggested to them that their lives, too, were influenced by forces beyond their personal control.

The wealthy, moreover, found it difficult to escape the pluralism that lay outside their immediate neighborhoods. Regular commuting on public conveyances to their business and leisure centers in the central business district took the rich through the Zone and slums and reminded them of the persistence of poverty, crime, congestion, ethnic and racial diversity, and class divisions. In addition, few of the upper-income areas were absolutely homogeneous. Members of "old" families often shared a street, schoolroom, or membership in a business association or women's club with some of the new rich, including increasing numbers of Catholics and Reform Jews and an occasional new immigrant, none of whom could trace their arrival in the United States beyond 1840. While the juxtaposition of these elements seldom produced serious ethnic or religious conflict among the residents of the periphery, intergroup relations in silk-stocking society tended to be cool, and social life cliquish.

The inhabitants of the suburban fringe, then, did not live beyond the reach of the city's problems or its flux and complexity, and they responded to their insecurity by establishing a web of professional, religious, civic, and social organizations whose goals varied. Some organizations, like the country club, were merely social and, by providing centers for family recreation, helped overcome geographic barriers to neighborliness imposed by the dispersal of high society. But local improvement associations sought to preserve real estate values and police protection in particular districts, and lawyers' and doctors' organizations, like the merchants' and manufacturers' associations, looked after the city-wide economic interests of their members while providing males with exclusive domains within which to enjoy the pleasures of genteel clubiness. Still other groups, including women's civic organizations and a broad range of church-related clubs, provided outlets for humanitarian impulses and agencies through which crime, disease, pollution, and other problems that affected all segments of society could be attacked.

Through all these organizations, irrespective of their specific goals, ran a strain of boosterism, the virulence of which hinted at the groups' underlying insecurity, defensiveness, and sense that the problems of the modern city called for heroic action. In 1905 the president of the Cincinnati Business Men's Club articulated this "whistling in the dark" attitude by reminding the membership that "Cincinnati is undergoing a great transformation" and by urging them to recognize that "we . . . must keep our municipality abreast [of] the times by cultivating civic patriotism and concentrating our energies for the upbuilding and uplifting of our beloved city."[8] That year, too, the Club adopted an official song.

> Circled by Ohio's waters
> Guarded by her hills
> Lies our dear old Cincinnati
> Fair her vision thrills
> Proudly may we tell thy story
> Heroes lived for thee. . . .

Nobly rise the years before thee
Victory beckons thee
For thine honor and thine glory,
We, thy sons, are one.

CONFUSION AND CONFLICT

The new city, with its tripartite residential configuration imposed upon a maze of ethnic, occupational, and class and status divisions, was a divided and volatile entity in which every segment of the urban population had to adjust to novel conditions of life. Simultaneous changes in the larger society generated anxieties that made that adjustment more difficult. The filling out of the continental system of cities ended the process of opening new urban and rural frontiers in unsettled regions and contributed to the growing feeling that the United States no longer promised the freedom, opportunity, and adventure of its less urban past. The shift of the economy into the mass production, industrial stage fed that fear, for the big corporations wielded economic influence, seemingly unlimited, which dwarfed that of small businessmen, urban workers, and farmers and undermined the old belief in the possibility of upward social and economic mobility. At the same time the continued diversification of the population through the advent of the "new" immigration weakened the old view of America as a melting pot capable of absorbing people of diverse backgrounds without destroying the essential unity of the nation's culture. Finally, the persisting flight from the farms to the cities eroded the traditional faith in the independent and sturdy yeoman farmer as the chief source and conservator of American ideals, and also fostered a deep-seated suspicion and resentment of city dwellers among those who remained in the countryside.

Capital vs. Labor

Coupled with the crisis of confidence in old ideals, changes in the 1880s and 1890s in the basic structure of the nation's cities and the socioeconomic system created widespread confusion and conflict. One line of contention ran between labor and management. Collisions between capital and labor had been common since 1820, but the general sense of insecurity associated with the opening of the urban-industrial era and the emergence of large classes of factory laborers and skilled

87

workers to whom the avenues of social and economic opportunity seemed irrevocably blocked broadened the scope and scale and increased the frequency of these clashes. Between 1883 and 1885 the economy skidded downward, and a surge of labor militancy spread across the country. In New York and Cincinnati, labor candidates came within an ace of capturing city hall, and workers in cities around the nation struck and boycotted to secure the eight-hour day, improved working conditions, and better pay. In 1886 alone over 600,000 men were out of work because of strikes or lockouts. Fear of the growing popularity of radical doctrines intensified and spread during the spring of that year after a bomb killed a policeman and six other persons during an anarchist rally in Chicago's Haymarket Square to protest police brutality.

Though tension eased as economic conditions improved during the late 1880s, industrial conflict resumed and the sense of crisis mounted with the onset of a deeper depression in the 1890s. That decade witnessed some of the most violent strikes in American history, including outbreaks at the Homestead plant of United States Steel Corporation in

48 and 49 On facing page, Federal troops guard a train during the Pullman Strike in 1894; at right, Coxey's Army on the march to Washington in the same year.

Pennsylvania and the Pullman Car Company in south suburban Chicago, both of which climaxed with confrontations between the police and federal troops on one side and strikers and their sympathizers on the other. As in the 1880s, moreover, many urban workers also turned to political action. This time, however, their attention centered not on municipal politics, but on demands for the adoption of a national public works program. To dramatize that proposal, Jacob S. Coxey of Massillon, Ohio, organized a massive march of the unemployed on Washington, D.C. As "Coxey's army" proceeded eastward, nervous local officials hastily improvised emergency measures to protect their cities from the vandalism, theft, and workingmen's violence that they felt the appearance of the marchers would surely bring. Little disruption attended the march, however, and Washington police banned the men from the city, herded them into camps on the outskirts of town, and arrested Coxey for walking on the grass.

89

Nativist vs. Immigrant

Analyzed in terms of the socioeconomic geography of cities, the industrial warfare of the late nineteenth century pitted the upper-income districts of the periphery of the city against the middle- and lower-middle-income areas of the Zone of Emergence. Yet residents of the Zone and the outer wards often lined up together in the second major conflict that wracked the country during these years. The general insecurity and sense of drift combined with the influx of immigrants from southern and eastern Europe deepened ethnic antipathies in the 1880s and 1890s, and it was in this conflict that the two peripheral districts tended to unite against the center. Caught up in the crisis of confidence, otherwise reasonable men placed the entire onus for the disrupted state of society and the economy on the "new" immigrants huddled in the slums of the inner city.

Many wealthy and old-stock big-city newspaper editors stereotyped the newcomers mercilessly and called for federal legislation placing restrictions on immigration. One denounced the newcomers as "rag-tag and bob-tail cutthroats of Beelzebub . . . , the very scum and offal of the earth." The country, wrote another, was undergoing "an invasion of

50 and 51 Two late-nineteenth-century expressions of nativist sentiment: On facing page, a view of the effect on "our peaceful rural districts" should the "Russian exodus of the persecuted Hebrews continue." At right, the caption comments on Irish immigration: "The balance of trade with Great Britain seems to be still against us."

venomous reptiles . . . , long-haired, wild-eyed, bad-smelling, atheistic, reckless foreign wretches, who never did an hour's work in their lives," and recommended that they be crushed "like snakes . . . , before they have a chance to bite." A third called immigration "a danger that threatens the destruction of our national edifice by the erosion of its moral foundations" and plumped for a "firm stand in favor of the right of Americans to govern Americans."[9]

In this atmosphere the lower-middle- and middle-class nativist organizations founded in the 1840s flourished once more. The Order of United American Mechanics, the Junior Order of United American Mechanics, and the Patriotic Sons of America broadened their memberships to include clerks, small merchants, and minor public functionaries as well as skilled workers. A host of new societies also sprang up. In 1886, the United Order of Deputies, later called the American League, appeared, and within four years the Minute Men of 1886, the American Patriotic League, the Loyal Men of America, and the Get There American Benefit Association joined the burgeoning list of nativist groups, all of which lumped immigrants, Catholicism, and radicalism as the chief threats to American society. The most influential of the new organizations was the APA, the American Protective Association. Like the others it drew its recruits and support from the cities as well as the countryside and exercised its political muscle largely within the Republican Party.

Interestingly enough, Protestant immigrants and second-generation newcomers played a significant role in these defenses of Americanism. Many apparently regarded nativist affiliation as one way of proving their loyalty and their right to belong beyond a doubt. But their relatively low position in the social and economic structure made them particularly vulnerable to feelings of insecurity and often forced them to compete directly with the most recent arrivals for jobs and housing.

Country vs. City: The Populists

The third major split within American society in the late nineteenth century developed out of the growing disparity between urban and rural life. In the late 1880s and early 1890s the old division between country and city, blunted during the middle decades of the century by the sectional dispute between the North and the South, emerged as a significant factor in national politics and produced a farmer's revolt. The continued flow of young people off the farms and into the cities, the heightened visibility of urban dominance, and the reduction in both the material rewards and social status of agriculture, especially among the smaller and more backward farmers of the South and West, generated a surge of rural antiurbanism that reached its apex with the Populist uprising of the 1890s. Though the People's Party platform of 1892 raised real economic grievances and contained planks designed to attract urban working-class support, Populist orators launched repeated attacks on the city. As one urban historian has put it, the embattled farmers "compiled a long list of enemies, some real, some imagined—Wall Street, Monopolists, Bankers, Foreigners, Catholics, Jews . . . ," all of whom "found a special home in the city."[10]

OTHER MANIFESTATIONS

Toward the end of the 1890s the Democratic Party made a special effort to capitalize on the farmers' discontent. William Jennings Bryan caught the bitterness of the rural reaction, became its most influential political symbol, and made the Democratic Party its political vehicle. A spokesman for those who believed in what Brand Whitlock disdainfully called "the moral superiority of the hayseed," Bryan also championed a theory of economic growth that denied the importance of the cities. "Burn down your cities and leave our farms," he told the 1896 Democratic convention, which nominated him for President, "and your cities will spring up again as if by magic; but destroy our farms and grass will grow in the streets of every city in the country."[11]

Bryan lost that campaign to William McKinley, and the election signaled the opening of a new era in the nation's political history. American politics had been in disarray since the 1840s and 1850s. Those years, as Arthur Schlesinger, Jr., recently summarized it, were times of "a desperate racial question . . . , rapid population growth, an unpopular war [with Mexico], mediocre political leadership, an outburst of native Americanism, an urban crisis, a spread of communes, a contagion of violence, a time of the disintegration of traditional parties, of multiple presidential candidates, of political division, evasion and drift."[12] Matters improved very little during the 1860s and 1870s. Although the GOP controlled the White House from 1868 to 1884, it could

52   Antiurbanism in 1890: the Farmers' Alliance mows down the politicians, among them representatives of the major parties.

not gather a congressional majority potent enough to resolve the racial crisis of the post–Civil War years or to deal with the paradox of poverty amidst unmatched economic productivity during this Gilded Age, as it had come to be called. But in the late nineteenth century the stalemate broke and the balance of political power tipped in favor of the Republicans.

Ascendancy of the GOP

Always strong in the small towns and the countryside, the Republicans now gathered strength in the cities. In the presidential elections of the 1880s most cities outside the South with a population of 50,000 or more went Republican. This trend continued, and in the Bryan-McKinley campaign of 1896, the GOP carried 70 of the 82 cities with populations over 45,000, including New York; 7 of the 12 cities in that rank went to Bryan were in the South. Even cities that had remained Democratic in the 1880s—San Francisco, Detroit, Indianapolis, Columbus, and St. Paul—voted Republican in 1896 and remained in the GOP column for several decades. Indeed, the Republican Party, building on an urban base, not only emerged as the national majority party in these years but held that position into the 1930s.

Several factors account for the GOP's success in the cities during the late nineteenth century: It took positions on several issues that made it especially attractive to voters in the outer wards. Its strong tariff stand pleased both industrialists seeking to exclude foreign competition and factory workers concerned about the threat of unemployment and low wages that free trade implied. By championing the gold standard and opposing the free coinage of silver as inflationary, the Republican Party also appealed to a broad range of urban consumers who worried about the high cost of living. A few prominent Republicans, moreover, like the Cleveland industrialist Mark Hanna, advocated the recognition of organized labor, and a coterie of eastern Republicans, followers of Senator Henry Cabot Lodge of Massachusetts, argued for immigration restriction in the 1890s and helped identify the GOP as a sympathetic haven for nativists.

Recent scholarship suggests a less tangible but nonetheless important sentiment that also pushed the urban vote toward the Republican column—the longing for a clear sense of direction and forceful leadership created by the emergence of the new city and the accompanying great economic and demographic changes. As the crisis of confidence mounted in the 1880s and 1890s, distraught city dwellers felt the need for a strengthened national government. While the Democrats clung to their traditional position of a limited role for the federal government, the GOP's brief history provided it with the image of the party of change, energy, and positive government. At mid-century Republicans had advocated the use of federal power to foster national economic growth by supporting the Homestead Act, federal subsidies for railroads, and a protective tariff. During the Civil War and Reconstruction, moreover, Republican administrations had abolished slavery, imposed federal income and inheritance taxes, and, through the Freedmen's Bureau, experimented with a nationally sponsored welfare program. And in the 1880s the leading spokesmen for federal aid to education were Republicans.

Not surprisingly, then, as city dwellers confronted the novel set of problems and strange environment of the new city and the corporate economy, they turned to the GOP for leadership. And from the 1890s into the 1950s one party or the other managed to dominate the federal government over long periods of time by commanding the urban vote. Whether these administrations were Republican or Democratic, the key to their success was the ability to persuade the urban electorate that they stood for a vigorous exercise of federal authority, not the older tradition of limited and weak central government. Thus urbanization in the mid- and late nineteenth century not only shattered the historic walking city, filled out the continental pattern of urban distribution, and revolutionized the economy, it also spawned a new urban-centered system of national politics, ushered in thirty years of Republican dominance, and created the conditions under which the federal government expanded its powers and eventually became a central force in American life.

Notes

[1] Quoted in David M. Potter, *People of Plenty: Economic Abundance and the American Character* (Chicago: The Univ. of Chicago Press, 1963), pp. 170–71.
[2] *Ibid.*, pp. 171–72.
[3] Quoted in Wade, "The City in History," p. 70.

[4] Quoted in Zane L. Miller, *Boss Cox's Cincinnati: Urban Politics in the Progressive Era* (New York: Oxford Univ. Press, 1968), p. 28.

[5] Quoted in Zane L. Miller, "Boss Cox and the Municipal Reformers: Cincinnati Progressivism, 1880–1914," Vol. I (Ph.D. dissertation, Univ. of Chicago, 1966), p. 39.

[6] *Ibid.*, p. 94.

[7] *Ibid.*, p. 98.

[8] Quoted in Miller, Vol. II, "Boss Cox," p. 405.

[9] Quoted in John Higham, *Strangers in the Land: Patterns of American Nativism, 1860–1925* (New York: Atheneum, 1963), pp. 54–55.

[10] Quoted in Wade, p. 70.

[11] *Ibid.*, p. 71.

[12] *The New Republic,* CLXIV (June 5, 1971), 25.

Bibliography

Chudacoff, Howard P. *Mobile Americans: Residential and Social Mobility in Omaha. 1880–1920.* New York: Oxford Univ. Press, 1972. A careful study that not only suggests that turn-of-the-century cities contained an extraordinarily mobile population, but also explores some important social and political consequences of high geographic mobility.

Cross, Robert D., ed. *The Church and the City.* Indianapolis and New York: Bobbs-Merrill, 1967. A collection of documents on Protestant churches in the modern city that contains an important introductory essay by the author.

Degler, Carl. "American Political Parties and the Rise of the City: An Interpretation," *Journal of American History.* LI (June, 1964), 41–59. Analyzes election trends and makes a case for the critical importance of the urban vote after the late nineteenth century.

McKelvey, Blake. *The Urbanization of America, 1860–1915.* New Brunswick, N.J.: Rutgers Univ. Press, 1963. Examines almost every aspect of city life in careful detail and contains an exhaustive bibliography.

Miller, Zane L. *Boss Cox's Cincinnati: Urban Politics in the Progressive Era.* New York: Oxford Univ. Press, 1968. The first three chapters examine patterns of growth in turn-of-the-century Cincinnati.

Wade, Richard C. "Violence in the Cities: A Historical View," in *Urban Violence.* Chicago: The Univ. of Chicago Center for Policy Study, 1969. The best brief summary of violence in American cities.

Warner, Sam Bass, Jr. *Streetcar Suburbs: The Process of Growth in Boston, 1870–1900.* New York: Atheneum, 1969. The best study of the impact of the new transportation technology on urban form.

———. *The Private City: Philadelphia in Three Periods of Its Growth.* Philadelphia: Univ. of Pennsylvania Press, 1968. Bears the marks of the "new nostalgia," yet presents a scaffolding for "inside" American urban history that supplements that of Richard C. Wade.

Wiebe, Robert. *The Quest for Order, 1877–1920.* New York: Hill and Wang, 1967. An especially imaginative general survey of the period.

Woods, Robert A. and Albert S. Kennedy. *The Zone of Emergence.* Abridged and edited by Sam B. Warner, Jr. Cambridge, Mass.: M.I.T. Press, 1962. An analysis of the Zone of Emergence in Boston by the originators of the concept.

part two

STABILIZATION

The New Urban Politics: 4
Bossism, Reform, and
the New City, 1880–1930

The gradual emergence of positive government at the national level after 1880 was paralleled by a similar development in the cities. During the middle decades of the nineteenth century local politicians often sought to create but seldom managed to sustain urban political systems capable of providing forceful and disciplined leadership for the cities. Several factors helped paralyze the political process, including the tangled structure of local government, the inexperience of political leaders in forging masses of voters into reliable coalitions, the social tensions engendered by the compression of people within the tight confines of the walking city, the disruption of old patterns of life during the first stages of industrialization, and the disorientation and confusion associated with large foreign immigration and rural-to-urban migration. By the early twentieth century, however, urban politics had grown more stable and municipal government more effective. Between 1880 and 1900 the forces that broke the mid-nineteenth-century political paralysis and sustained the early-twentieth-century urban renaissance took shape.

INTENSIFICATION OF CRISIS

As the modern city emerged in the last two decades of the nineteenth century the urban crisis deepened. Appallingly high levels of residential congestion in the central city exacerbated health hazards long associated with urban life. The clash of cultures between ethnic ghettos within the central city and along the cutting edge of the swelling slums set off riots and acrimonious controversies among religious, ethnic, and neighborhood factions. Strikes regularly erupted into violence, and elections, as in the past, frequently degenerated into brutal brawls. With the rapid expansion in the physical area of the city, moreover, residents of the newer neighborhoods demanded new or improved gas, electric, water, sewer, police, fire, education, and health services, yet insisted that tax levels be kept low.

The intensification of the urban crisis in the late nineteenth century convinced a wide range of politically active citizens that city politics would have to be stabilized and municipal government centralized in order to control the disorder created by the emergence of the new city. But few agreed on the vital question of how urban politics and government could be made more effective and responsive. Broadly speaking, two strategies appeared: one was championed by a new and more effective generation of bosses, the other by a diverse set of self-styled reformers.

THE NEW BOSSES

The new bosses, like their less successful mid-nineteenth-century predecessors, sought to make city administrations more positive by creating an "invisible" bureaucracy to cut through the red tape and secure the cooperation of elected and appointed officials in the tangled maze of municipal government. Built around either the Republican or Democratic Party apparatus, the "machine" pyramided from a grass-roots base in the wards and precincts to its peak in the leader's office at party headquarters. The techniques for developing and mobilizing such an organization differed very little from those used by Tweed and others in the mid-nineteenth century. But after 1880, machine politicians in city after city acquired enough influence to make creaky municipal governments function in a constructive way.

Power Sources

The new strength of the bosses derived from the enlarged bureaucracy and new residential configuration created by the geographic explosion of cities. The expansive tendency of the modern city required the extension of old and the introduction of new city services, and as the size and scope of city governments mounted, key officials accumulated

53 Comment on "Boss" Tweed's gift of $50,000 to the poor of his ward. Entitled "Tweedledee and Sweedledum (A New Christmas Pantomime at the Tammany Hall)," it has Tweed saying: "Let's blind them with this, and then take some more." Sweedledum is probably a reference to Peter Sweeney who was county treasurer during Tweed's reign.

a new range of power, which derived from their newly enlarged stock of patronage with which to reward faithful party workers. Thus they could direct the distribution of lucrative construction and supply contracts and streetcar, gas, electric light, and telephone franchises to those who either worked for, contributed to, or cooperated with the machine. They could also juggle tax assessments of commercial firms, industries, and residential property owners, exert pressure on banks eager for city deposits, dispense juicy printing accounts, plant tips among friendly real estate operators about future public improvements that would affect property values, provide part-time employment for struggling young doctors or lawyers, and persuade the police, judges, and other city officials to protect favored special interests, including gambling and prostitution. The skillful orchestration of these rewards gave astute political operators powerful leverage with which to line up support among and secure the cooperation of large numbers of lower-middle-, middle-, and upper-income residents in the Zone of Emergence and the outer wards.

To take advantage of these broadened sources of municipal influence, however, the boss had to acquire a hold on the appropriate appointed or elected officeholder. The boss's "clout," therefore, depended in the final analysis on his ability to deliver regularly a bloc of voters large enough to affect decisively the outcome of city elections. The residential structure of the modern city made that task easier than ever, for after 1880 the densest accumulation of voters was the poor, conveniently herded into broad slums that spanned the numerous older and smaller wards of the central city. Here lived the voters who most desperately needed help, and the bosses' special genius lay in their ability to activate and organize the potential political power of the poor and uprooted masses of the inner neighborhoods. Their numbers comprised their only strength, and every city possessed a cadre of politicians who stood quite ready to ride that strength into city hall.

The boss had much to offer in return for the vote of the slum dweller, his family, friends, and neighbors. To the poor and the newcomers of the central city the machine supplied public jobs or private employment with a firm friendly to the organization, coal and rent money in bad times, outings to the country or an outlying amusement park dur-

54 "Boss" Croker of New York prepares to distribute his patronage among the politically loyal.

ing the pitiless heat of a long city summer, legal aid and advice, foreign-language classes in the schools, and the assurance that the special holidays, religious festivities, and Old World customs of the foreign-born would be protected from the attacks of nativists and moralistic crusaders. Equally important, turning out the vote for the organization gave the poor and the despised immigrant the status and satisfaction of holding a party position or public office (albeit low-level), and voting for machine candidates gave those at the bottom of urban society the chance, for once, to be on the winning side. Frequently a slum resident himself, the aspiring boss first lined up the solid support of a precinct, then a ward, and eventually of whole central-city neighborhoods. He then fished among the various interest groups of the Zone and suburban fringe for allies to finance the organization and carry city-wide elections. Occasionally a boss took over after lining up just one or two central-city districts, but he found it easy to expand his support there. In the slums the boss found his most steady and reliable support, and by the repeated improvisation of diverse coalitions resting on a central-city base the machine contrived to hold power long enough to get things done.

103

Yet the power of the boss, while formidable, was never absolute. He always had to deliver for his varied clientele, and perpetually he faced challenges from reform forces. Though most machine leaders sought to mute antiboss criticism by adopting reform proposals that least offended the central-city organization constituency, a deep-rooted antipathy between reformers and bosses made any alliance of the two forces extremely tenuous. Upper-income residents of the urban fringe led the reform forces, and their major aim, stated in its most general form, was to reach long-range and abstract goals such as "purifying" municipal government or providing for the general welfare by making the city safer, healthier, and more prosperous. The bosses, by contrast, were tied more closely to a different constituency and had to respond to the immediate economic needs of their less affluent clientele.

REFORM

Efficiency lay at the heart of the varied reform programs, and broad-based support within the peripheral districts gave the movement strength and persistence. Businessmen who commuted from suburban residences to their downtown stores and offices found quite obvious the connection between central-business-district congestion, inadequate fire and police protection, jammed intraurban transport systems and high insurance rates, lost time and energy, and increasing property taxes. Suburban women, partially released from a full-time commitment to home, husband, and children by technological aids to housework, by trends toward smaller dwellings and families, and by broadened access to postsecondary education also joined in the civic uplift drive. But their interests ran more along humanitarian lines, looking to the creation of an urban socioeconomic system that offered the poor and the newcomers a variety of paths up and out of the slums. Instead, however, of offering direct economic aid to the poor, they set out to improve the physical, educational, and moral environments so that slum dwellers and the lower-middle class could pull themselves up by their own bootstraps. Toward that end this wing of the reform movement sought to expand public health services and facilities, locate and design parks to meet the needs of all the people, establish playgrounds, reconstruct the educational system to prepare young and old alike for rewarding jobs and active participation in civic life, and improve the physical environment of slum life, particularly housing. Other reformers felt, in addition, that elimination of vice and crime deserved a high priority. A diverse array of suburban males supported these programs, including enlightened businessmen and socially conscious lawyers, physicians, journalists, educators, and religious leaders. So did smaller but equally varied contingents of Zone residents, although in that district spokesmen for organized labor played the most conspicuous role. For these diverse groups reform became an instrument of social control, a means to impose order upon the distended cities and reduce the chasm between the culture of the periphery and that of the center.

Generally, the reform movement in any given place proceeded through two phases. At first the emphasis fell on private, voluntary efforts, and produced a maze of new agencies and organizations designed both to alert the residents of the periphery to the nature and urgency of the crisis and to establish institutional outlets for action. Businessmen's organizations studied municipal conditions in search of sources of economic inefficiency, and women's groups set up kindergartens, summer vacation schools, neighborhood parks and playgrounds for slum youth, and opened publicity campaigns against poor housing, unsanitary conditions, and smoke problems. Welfare reformers created city-wide relief agencies, and all three major religions established central-city "institutional" churches that offered vocational training, advice on health care and household management, and meeting rooms for youth groups and adult clubs. Settlement houses, under both religious and secular auspices, provided similar services and permitted middle-class volunteers to experience slum life firsthand while giving slum dwellers a closer look at the values, attitudes, and skills the strangers from the periphery brought to the problems of the center. Physicians persuaded hospitals to undertake follow-up social work with central-city patients and their families. And so it went, with each perceived problem coming under attack from one or another private organization. By the turn of the century reformers in every major city felt compelled to print fat manuals listing the officers, addresses, and services available among the welter of social and civic agencies.

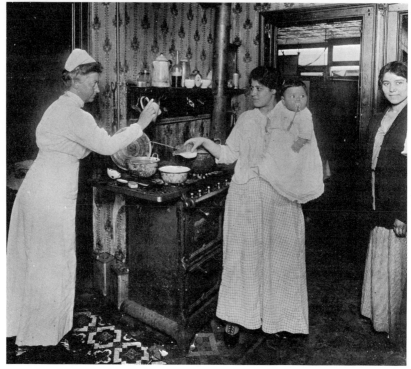

55 A visiting nurse instructs an immigrant mother in the care of her baby in a carefully posed promotional picture made at the turn of the century.

During its second phase the civic uplift movement gathered momentum and centered its energies on politics. One of the chief objectives in this stage was to add successful private programs to the growing battery of services offered by municipalities. But the major commitment was to centralize, democratize, and purify city government by eliminating bossism. Some reformers worked within the major parties; others turned to nonpartisan politics and the creation of local third parties. Whatever their tactics, however, their primary target remained the boss and machine politics.

Opponents of bossism resented the machine for several reasons. Reformers deplored the patronage system as inefficient and decried the "honest graft" implicit in the machine's deals with business groups and the dishonest graft of franchise-jobbing and protection-peddling as fraudulent, illegal, and immoral. Other antimachine critics feared the influence that immigrants exercised on city politics through connections with the organization and detested the bosses' penchant for filling "experts'" jobs in the municipal bureaucracy with ill-educated and partially qualified men. Still others, impressed by the efficiency of big business corporations, hoped to streamline city government and dismantle the machine in one stroke by junking ward representation. These "structural reformers" preferred to centralize the city administration and reduce the influence of ward politicians by adopting the small council-city manager, commission, or strong mayor form of government and a vigorous civil service system. These measures, they contended, would eliminate the need for "invisible" government through the neighborhood-based party bureaucracy and would reshape city government in the image of the corporation, with department heads responsible to a few talented members on the "board of directors" at the top. Democracy, they argued, could be preserved under this system by assuring voters the power to recall officials, to adopt legislation, and to reconsider controversial acts by officials.

56   The merit system in one of its earliest applications to government employment: Civil Service job applicants undergo examination in New York City in 1879.

Buttressed by nonpartisan "Committees of 100," which operated chiefly in the more thinly settled and larger wards of the periphery, the reformers launched repeated attacks on the machine and, by implication, on the bosses' most steadfast supporters in the central city. In some cities the contest between bossism and reform was played out on fairly equal terms, but in most the bosses clearly held the edge. After 1880, men like William Crump in Memphis, Martin Behrman in New Orleans, the Pendergast brothers in Kansas City, Missouri, Abraham Reuf in San Francisco, Charles Croker in New York, and George B. Cox in Cincinnati put together cohesive organizations and forged majorities capable of running the city. Indeed, it was not unusual for one boss to remain the dominant political factor in one city for an entire generation.

MACHINE AND REFORM: INTERPLAY IN CINCINNATI

Impressed by the bosses' durability, Lincoln Steffens and a host of turn-of-the-century observers in every city depicted bossism as a tyrannical, corrupt, relentlessly efficient (in furthering its own interests), and virtually invulnerable political juggernaut. On the whole they were right. But these critics obscured as much as they revealed about urban politics after 1880. In even the most machine-ridden places the boss comprised but one part of the novel political system of the new city. From San Francisco to New Orleans to New York the interplay of machine and reform elements provided the basis for the emergence of strengthened city governments and a revitalization of the political system that sustained a remarkable urban renaissance throughout the first three decades of the twentieth century. Though the unfolding of the pattern varied from place to place, the history of machine politics in Cincinnati illustrates the process in a city that experienced the chaotic disorder of the late nineteenth century, passed through a prolonged period of boss rule by a Republican machine in the early twentieth century, and witnessed a clear-cut reform victory in the 1920s.

In the 1880s Cincinnati, like most American cities, had entered the final stages of its transformation from a historic walking city into a modern urban center. The immediate impact of the emergence of the

57　A lynch mob storms the county jail in Cincinnati in 1884.

new city pushed Cincinnati to the brink of anarchy. In March 1884, the Cincinnati *Enquirer* complained that the police had failed to choke off a crime wave although, in the last year alone, there had been 12 arrests for malicious shooting, 29 for malicious cutting, 47 for cutting with intent to wound, 284 for shooting with intent to kill, 92 for murder and manslaughter, and 948 for carrying a concealed weapon. The total number of arrests came to 56,784 in a city with a total population of 250,000. Later that same month, a lynch mob descended on the county jail. While police and militia fought off the mob, gangs looted stores and shops on the fringe of the downtown district. In three days of riot the courthouse was burned to the ground, 54 people were killed, and an estimated 200 people were wounded. During the fall elections, violence erupted in the lower wards; two policemen and one black man were killed. Congressman Benjamin Butterworth remarked that he had "never witnessed anywhere such coarse brutality and such riotous demonstrations. . . ." Cincinnati, he concluded, "seems . . . doomed to perdition."[1]

These spectacular outbreaks plus other pressures overwhelmed city hall. Indeed, scarcely a residential area, economic interest, or social or occupational group was left unscathed by the multidimensional disorder. Here, as elsewhere, citizens of recently annexed districts deluged officials with proposals for the extension, improvement, and inauguration of public services and for lower taxes. At the same time deterioration of older neighborhoods and the relative decline of the city in regional economic importance heightened the urgency of the agitation for a positive and forceful response to the crisis.

The new city, with old ways shattered, made a fertile breeding ground for turmoil and discontent, but it also provided a challenge and an opportunity for those seeking innovation and creative reconstruction. Initially, however, this unprecedented rate of change accompanied by unprecedented demands for government action produced only the hope

58 The Republican Party, through the Blaine Club, raises the banner of reform in Cincinnati in 1899.

DEMOCRACY'S BANNER

"FOR TWO YEARS WE HAVE ADMINISTERED FROM THE HIGHEST TO THE LOWEST, FROM MAYOR TO JANITOR, THE ADMINISTRATIVE OFFICES OF THIS CITY FAITHFULLY AND WELL."

FIDELITY TO THE INTERESTS OF ALL THE PEOPLE AND JEALOUS DEVOTION TO THEM AND THEIR AFFAIRS HAVE BEEN THE WELL-KEPT PLEDGES OF FAITHFUL PUBLIC SERVANTS

YOUNG MEN'S BLAINE CLUB

Dear Sir:

The local Democracy has raised its banner proclaiming the issue upon which the present Municipal Campaign shall be fought. In the Convention which named the Democratic Candidates for Members of the B. C. A., the Chairman declared Democracy's faith in Democratic Administration of the City's affairs, and his words quoted above were applauded to the echo. The Republican Party accepts this issue and the Young Men's Blaine Club presents a picture portraying the conditions which the Democratic Convention endorsed and which it expects the citizens of Cincinnati to approve. Cincinnatians are invited to pass judgment. Be sure to vote. Vote the Republican Ticket. Vote to rebuke false pretenses, inefficiency, mis-management and mal-administration.

Election, Monday, April 3d.

POLLS CLOSE AT 4 O'CLOCK P. M.

Respectfully,
HARRY M. HOFFHEIMER, Chairman,
FRANK S. KRUG,
WM. LITTLEFORD,
ADOLPH GEIGER,
Election Committee, Y. M. B. C.

Cincinnati, March 23, 1899.

for improvement. Throughout the 1880s no party could put together a decisive ruling majority, and the city's political processes remained frozen.

Boss Cox

By 1897, however, all this had changed. In January of that year, three months before the city election, the Cincinnati *Post* gravely announced its intention to describe "impassionately and without bias the means employed" in what it sarcastically described as Cincinnati's "superior and unrecorded government." That government was controlled by "the boss, whose power is absolute"—George B. Cox.

The *Post's* analysis of bossism in Cincinnati closely paralleled those of other machine enemies in other cities. It dissected the patronage system, outlined the sources of financial support, and noted the special appeals made to the city's various special groups—the veterans (of the Civil War), the Germans, the Republican clubs, the Reform Jews, the legal and medical professions, the socially prominent businessmen from the suburban fringe, and certain cooperative Democrats. It excitedly reported the effectiveness of the organization's intelligence system, the way the "plugger" and the "knocker" wore "beaten paths to the office of the boss to urge the appointment of this man, the discharge of that or to report some feature of misconduct or expression [of dissatisfaction] . . . ." The paper noted that Cox was always available for consultation with any citizen regardless of station or status, and that he had been little more than one of several important factional leaders until, in 1886, Governor Joseph B. Foraker selected him to serve as chief advisor on patronage and political affairs in Hamilton County.

Foraker made a shrewd choice, for Cox had grown up with the city and received a liberal education in its ways. The son of British immigrants, he was born in 1853 and reared in the Eighteenth Ward, a declining central-city district that, by the 1880s, contained fashionable as well as slum housing, factories, and its share of saloons and brothels. His father died when Cox was eight. Successively, Cox worked as a bootblack, newsboy, lookout for a gambling joint, grocery deliveryman, bartender, and tobacco salesman. His school principal, who later became superintendent of schools, claimed that Cox was frequently in boyish trouble in classes, exhibited an "undisguised love for his mother," and "never lied . . . bore malice, sulked, whined or moped." Cox had also been exposed to religion. Although not a churchgoer, as an adult he had, according to one journalist, "dormant powerful sentiments, which rest on foundations of the firmest faith."[2]

In the mid-1870s Cox acquired a saloon in his home neighborhood. He entered politics, rose to the top of the Eighteenth Ward organization, and served on the city council from 1878 until 1885 when, after joining forces with the Republican reform mayoralty candidate, he ran unsuccessfully for county clerk. He tried for the same post in 1888, failed, and never again stood for public office.

The Cox-GOP Axis

At that time, moving away politically from the slums, Cox worked with George Moerlein, a brewer and perhaps the strongest of the GOP professionals in the Zone of Emergence. In 1890, he and Moerlein quarreled over patronage, and in the city convention of 1891 Cox was able, with the support of the Blaine Club (a kind of political settlement house that he had helped to establish), to defeat Moerlein's candidate for police judge and nominate his own man. Moerlein men now became Cox men. So, too, did Charles P. Taft and the Cincinnati *Times-Star,* which had been one of the last, most influential, and most outspoken of Cox's critics in suburban Republican circles. The newspaper accepted Cox as party leader, it announced, in order to secure a "new order" for Cincinnati. And the president of the gas company, sensing the political drift, confided to his diary that he had "concluded [an] arrangement with Geo. B. Cox for services at $3500 per year quarterly to last for three years."[3] In the spring election of 1894, the Republicans carried the city with a plurality of over 6500 votes, the first decisive municipal election in a decade. In 1897 Cox was the honest broker in a coalition composed of central-city and Zone blacks, Zone politicians, the gas and traction companies, and Republican reformers from the outer wards.

Election returns after 1885 reveal the political and social geography of the Cox-Republican ascendancy. The GOP won five successive contests by uniting suburban support with enough strength in the Zone to overcome the Democratic grip on the slums. Until 1894, however, the

59 Comment on "Boss" Cox's control of Cincinnati political life, including nominations for office—up to and including that of mayor.

margins of victory were perilously thin. The substantial triumph of that year merely marked the completion of the alliance, which pitted a united periphery against the center of the city. The heart of the Republican "new order" coalition, and the critical factor in the election of 1894, was its appeal to voters in the suburban fringe, who demanded order and reform.

To satisfy the suburbs, Cox and his associates eliminated the ward "bummer" (who sold his influence to corrupt candidates), provided brief and decorous conventions, enfranchised blacks by suppressing antiblack violence at the polls, reduced the rapid turnover in office, and cut down the incidence of petty graft and corporation raiding. But the machine also heeded the advice of its reform allies from the suburbs in policy matters. Cox accepted the secret ballot, voter registration, and a series of state laws that, though retaining the major-council form of government with ward representation, were designed to give the city a

113

60 Wielert's beer garden, popular meeting place of many of Cox's lieutenants.

stable and more centralized government. The administrations endorsed by Cox started to build a professional police force, expanded and re-equipped the fire department, pushed through a $6 million water-works program, renovated municipal institutions, supported the growth of the University of Cincinnati, launched extensive street-paving and sewer-constructing projects, and tried to reduce the smoke problem and expand the city's park acreage. They also opened the door to housing regulation; tightened the controls on the Sunday saloon, flagrant public gambling, and disorderly brothels (the city was never really closed); began to bring order into the chaotic public utilities field by favoring privately owned, publicly regulated monopolies under progressive management; and succeeded in keeping the tax rate low. The Republican regime, in short, brought positive government to Cincinnati.

While this program also won votes in the Zone, it was not the sole basis for the party's popularity there. Many of the lieutenants and captains closest to Cox were Zone residents. They composed a colorful group known variously as "the gang," "the sports," or the "bonifaces"—a clique that met nightly in the Zone either at the Schubert and Pels saloon, where each had a personal beer mug with his name gilded on

114

it, or at the round table in Wielert's beer garden. Three of them owned or operated combination saloons, gambling joints, and dance halls; one was prominent in German charitable associations and the author of several textbooks used in the elementary schools; another served twenty consecutive terms as president of the Hamilton County League of Building Associations; and one was a former catcher for the Cincinnati Redlegs. Their tastes, behavior, and attitudes were summarized in the sketches of ward leaders and city officials in the 1901 *Police and Municipal Guide.* They were characterized as friendly, well-known, "All Around Good-Fellows" who belonged to several social and fraternal groups, gave generously to charity, and showered the poor and sick with special kindness. They were all among the most ardent supporters of any project to boost the city.

Cox is pictured in the *Guide* as an adherent to the code of the Zone who had risen to the top. He was a bon vivant who enjoyed good cigars and good jokes, a man of wealth whose recently completed mansion in the bucolic fringe neighborhood of Clifton was luxuriously decorated and adorned with expensive works of art, a man of impressive but quiet and private charity. Above all he was true to his word, loyal to his friends, yet quick to reprimand and replace those who betrayed his trust by misusing public office.

Cox and his top civil servants—surrounded by a motley crowd of newspaper reporters, former boxers and ball players, vaudeville and burlesque performers, and other Vine Street characters—provided an attractive model for men who yearned for the glamor, wealth, and power that was so visible yet so elusive in the new city. Cox's opponents in the Zone seldom attacked him or his inside group directly. Even in the heat of the 1897 campaign, the *Volksfreund,* the German Catholic Democratic daily, carefully described Cox as an "amiable man" who had to be "admired" for his "success" and, either ignoring or unaware of the process of negotiation and mediation by which Cox ruled, criticized him only for his illiberality in imposing "dictatorial methods" on the GOP. Indeed, most Zone residents, like those in the suburbs, found it difficult to object to a government that seemed, in contrast to those of the 1860s and 1870s, humane, efficient, and progressive.

Yet it would be a mistake to overestimate the strength of the "new

61 George Cox's residence, still standing today, in a suburb of Cincinnati.

order" Republican coalition. Its victories from 1885 to 1894 were won by close pluralities in three-way races. The organization, moreover, failed to carry a referendum for the sale of the city-owned Southern Railroad in 1896, lost the municipal contest in 1897 to a reform fusion ticket, and lost the fall elections of 1897, 1898, and 1899 to the Democrats. In all these reversals, crucial defections occurred in both the suburbs and the Zone. Skittish voters grew indignant over alleged corruption, outraged by inaction on promises to improve streetcar and gas service, piqued by the rising cost of new city projects, annoyed by the slow expansion of the educational program, or uneasy over the partial sacrifice of democracy to efficiency within the Republican organization.

Thereafter, however, the Republicans rallied and won three of the next four city elections by unprecedented margins. The strategy and tactics remained essentially the same. Although not wholly averse to raising national issues, Cox's group gave local affairs the most emphasis, The organization was occasionally purged of its less savory elements. Cox and his Zone advisors continued to consult with their suburban allies on nominations. The party promised and, in fact, tried to deliver order and reform. Without abolishing ward representation in the city council, it strengthened the mayor and streamlined the administration. The party also broadened and deepened its program as civic associations, women's clubs, social workers, social gospellers, and spokesmen for the new unionism—all novel forces in urban politics— expanded and elaborated their demands. But voting patterns underwent a fundamental change. By 1903 the Republicans dominated the entire city, carrying not only the Zone and suburbs, but also the city center. The slums were now the invincible bulwark of Cox's power.

Several factors were involved in the conversion of inner-city Democrats to Republicanism. First, Cox had extensive personal contacts with them that dated back to his unsuccessful races for county clerk in the 1880s. Second, the Democrats had been unable to put down factionalism. By the late 1890s there were two reform elements in the party, both of which belabored the regulars from the center of the city as tainted with corruption, too cozy with Cox, and perhaps worst of all, as a discredit and burden to the party because they wore the charred shirt of the courthouse riot.

In the wake of the fusionist victory of 1897, which pitted reform Democrats and independent Republicans from the periphery against

62 A campaign poster of 1907 links Cox with more illustrious ornaments of the Republican Party.

PRESIDENT ROOSEVELT.   HON. GEO. B. COX.   ABRAHAM LINCOLN.

OUR PEERLESS LEADERS.

VOTE THE TICKET STRAIGHT.

REMEMBER OUR CAMPAIGN BUTTON!

Nov. 5, 1907

63 Cox depicted in his role as dispenser of graft, in this case to keep his threatened political ship afloat.

the Cox organization, Mike Mullen, the leader of a riverfront Democratic ward in the heart of the city, explained to the *Enquirer* why he would henceforth work with the Republican party.

> I have worked hard [for the Democratic party] have suffered much and have won for it many victories. Yet all the while there was a certain element . . . that looked on me with distrust . . . Leaders of the Fusionist Party did not think enough of me to let me look after the voting in my own ward, but sent down a lot of people to watch the count. That decided me.[4]

He was later joined by Colonel Bob O'Brien who, like Mullen, specialized in Christmas turkey, soup-line, and family-service politics. These and other central-city Democratic politicians led their constituents into the Republican fold.

Decline

It was this alliance with the central city that ultimately destroyed Cox, for it enabled reformers to convince voters in the Zone and outer wards that Republican connections with the slums constituted an immoral and corrupt alliance that would ruin the city. A catalogue of complicated city problems could be summarized and dramatized by invoking the evil image of bossism, a formula that provided reformers a simple yet compelling appeal to unite the heterogeneous voters of the Zone and periphery. Antimachine spokesmen were convinced that they had to educate the city before they could redeem it, and they felt, too, that politics was a potent educational tool. But campaigns had to be spectacular in order to engage the voters' attention and participation. As A. Julius Freiberg noted, the "psychology" of the electorate was such that years of "speaking, writing, explaining, even begging and imploring" had been "to no purpose." The "reformer and his fellow students may sit about the table and evolve high principles for action, but the people . . . will not be fed by those principles unless there is a dramatic setting, and the favorite dramatic setting is the killing of a dragon." And all the people "love the dramatic; not merely the poor, but the rich, and the middle class as well." All that was needed was a situation that would enable the right man to "bring to book the boss himself."[5]

Reformers now hammered relentlessly at the theme that Cox was not a good boss and depicted him as the head of a "syndicate" that included the worst products of slum life. In "that part of the city where vice and infamy hold high revel," went one version of the charge, "the boss-made ticket finds its most numerous supporters. Every dive keeper, every creature who fattens upon the wages of sin . . . , all the elements at war with society have enlisted." Men "who claim to be respectable," the chief "beneficiaries of this unholy alliance . . . , go down into the gutter and accept office from hands that are reeking with the filth of the slums." Worse still, this "alliance of the hosts of iniquity with the greed of special privilege and ambition for power and place" plays so successfully "upon the prejudices and . . . superstition of the many that wrong is often espoused by those who in the end are the victims of the wrong."[6]

The reformers also impugned Cox's personal integrity. Democratic County Prosecutor Henry T. Hunt secured evidence that Cox had perjured himself in 1906 when he said he had not received a cent of some $250,000 of interest on public funds that Republican county treasurers had been paid by bankers. In the spring of 1911, Hunt and the grand

64 Henry T. Hunt, County Prosecutor in Cincinnati, who obtained an indictment against Cox and 123 associates in 1911.

jury indicted Cox and 123 others during a broad investigation of politics, corruption, and vice.

Finally, Hunt, stressing the issue of moral indignation, ran for mayor in the fall of 1911 on a Democratic reform ticket. Using the moral rhetoric of the muckraker, Hunt and his associates tied bossism, the chaos, poverty, and vice of the slums, and the malefactors of great wealth together and pictured them as a threat to the welfare of the whole city. Once again the suburban fringe and Zone voted for order and reform. Hunt's progressive coalition swept the periphery, lost only in the inner-city wards, and won the election.

By that time, however, Cox was no longer boss. President Taft and Charles P. Taft had wanted Cox to step aside as early as 1905, but they found him indispensable. After the grand-jury revelations, however, they were able to convince the "bonifaces" that Cox was a liability. With the organization against him Cox retired. For a time, he insisted that his two chief assistants, August Herrmann and Rudolph Hynicka, should also quit, apparently convinced that they, like himself, could no longer command the confidence of the periphery. Charles P. Taft's Cincinnati *Times-Star* agreed. The two men, backed by the Blaine Club, merely resigned their official party positions but refused to get out of politics entirely.

Cox's Role Reconsidered

What, then, was Cox's role in politics and government in the new city? He helped create and manage a voluntary political-action organization that bridged the racial and cultural chasms between the slums, Zone, and suburbs. He and his allies were able to bring positive and moderate reform government to Cincinnati and to mitigate the conflict and disorder that accompanied the emergence of the new city. With the crisis atmosphere muted, ardent reformers could develop more sophisticated programs and agitate, educate, and organize without arousing the kind of divisive, emotional, and hysterical response that had immobilized municipal statesmen in the mid-nineteenth century. In the process, while battering at the boss, the slums, and the special-privilege syndicate, they shattered the bonds of confidence that linked the Zone "bonifaces" and the moderate reformers of the suburbs to Cox's organization.

After the First World War, with Cox dead and his successor, Rudolph Hynicka, trying to run the machine from his theatrical offices in New York, the stage was set for a dramatic shift of power in Cincinnati. In the mid-1920s the reformers launched yet another attack on bossism. This time they managed not only to defeat the GOP but also to secure the adoption of the city manager plan of city government, a small (nine-man) city council elected at large, and a broadened civil service. These structural alterations provided a framework within which the forces of the periphery could more than hold their own in the persistent struggle between bossism and reform. From 1925 into the 1950s the nonpartisan Charter Party held the balance of power in Queen City politics. But in other larger places, which, unlike Cincinnati, grew rapidly or received more immigrants from southern and eastern Europe after 1900, the old struggle between the center and periphery continued on more even terms.

Notes

[1] Zane L. Miller, "Boss Cox's Cincinnati: A Study in Urbanization and Politics," *The Journal of American History*, LIV, 4 (March, 1968), pp. 823–38.
[2] *Ibid.*
[3] *Ibid.*
[4] *Ibid.*
[5] A. Julius Freiberg, "Mayor Hunt's Administration in Cincinnati," *National Municipal Review*, III (July, 1914), 517-18.
[6] Miller, "Boss Cox's Cincinnati."

Bibliography

Dorset, Lyle W. *The Pendergast Machine*. New York: Oxford Univ. Press, 1968. Particularly useful because it traces the growth and development of a machine from the turn of the century into the 1930s.

Callow, Alexander. *The Tweed Ring*. New York: Oxford Univ. Press, 1966. The most colorful and the only full-scale account of what the author calls the "most infamous city political machine in our history."

Holli, Melvin G. *Reform in Detroit: Hazen G. Pingree and Urban Politics*. New York: Oxford Univ. Press, 1968. An analysis of reform politics in Detroit that draws a useful distinction between structural and social reform.

Mandelbaum, Seymour. *Boss Tweed's New York*. New York: Wiley, 1965. Much shorter than Callow's study (above) and more sharply interpretive. Mandelbaum explains the Tweed phenomenon through the application of communications theory.

Miller, Zane L. *Boss Cox's Cincinnati: Urban Politics in the Progressive Era*. New York: Oxford Univ. Press, 1968. Treats reform and bossism as integral parts of the modern urban political system and places the dialectic in a center-periphery framework.

Stave, Bruce M. *Urban Bosses, Machines, and Progressive Reformers*. Lexington, Mass.: Heath, 1972. Provides a guide to the conflicting views of contemporaries and historians on turn-of-the-century city politics.

Tarr, Joel Arthur. *A Study in Boss Politics: William Lorimer of Chicago*. Urbana: Univ. of Illinois Press, 1971. Emphasizes the role of ethnocultural and religious factors in early-twentieth-century urban politics.

Builders of the Early- 5
Twentieth-Century City:
Chicago, 1900–1930

After the turn of the century, though economic forces and changing transportation and construction technologies continued to play an important role in molding urban form, the social geography and physical arrangement of cities were increasingly determined by a broad commitment to revitalize the sense of community that so many felt had evaporated with the late-nineteenth-century explosion in the scale of urban life. Since the builders and planners of the twentieth-century city came from all levels of urban society, their definitions of the appropriate territorial base on which to build community varied. Some chose a narrow definition that emphasized the importance of creating small and distinct socio-geographic entities, while others adopted a comprehensive view and sought means to infuse the metropolis as a whole with a sense of unity.

THE CITY: COMMUNITY OR COMMUNITIES?

At least five groups preferred a specialized land use pattern that would divide the metropolis into particular neighborhoods and districts. Urban newcomers and lower-middle- and middle-class native whites as well as second-generation immigrants tried to create small communities centered upon relatively homogeneous ethnic settlements. Annexationist politicians, by bringing city services to remote edges of the metropolis, helped create a layer of residential neighborhoods around the rim of more densely settled areas. Businessmen also fostered the development of small outlying subcenters by distributing commercial and industrial districts across the face of the metropolis while developing the central business district into a coordinating unit for the dispersed subunits. Some wealthy social reformers from peripheral wards sought to galvanize a sense of neighborhood solidarity in the inner city to help slum dwellers acquire the social, educational, and political prerequisites for socioeconomic mobility, while others constructed planned communities on the rim of metropolises.

Those who favored the development of a sense of metropolitan community also regarded themselves as reformers, and like other reformers they resided in outer districts. They hoped to devise metropolitan administrative mechanisms or to use comprehensive planning on a metropolitan scale to foster a city-wide feeling of civic cohesion and a neighborly, big community encompassing all the inhabitants of the metropolis. Though neighborhood and metropolitan planners sought to control the destiny of virtually every major city between 1900 and 1930, Chicago provides a luminous illustration of how cities grew as a result of the simultaneous emergence of advocates of both the small and big community among the builders of the twentieth-century city.

THE GROWTH OF CHICAGO:
ECONOMICS AND GEOGRAPHY

Chicago engaged the interest of the nation in the early twentieth century despite the fact that the most spectacular urban growth was occurring in places that capitalized upon new and specialized functions. The fastest-developing cities in the decade before 1930, for example, were Detroit, the automobile city; Akron, the country's leading rubber tire

65 South Water Street in Chicago in 1834. About a generation later the population of Chicago was nearly 300,000.

producer; Tulsa, Oklahoma City, and Houston, booming oil towns in the Southwest; Miami, the recreation and retirement paradise of the 1920s; and Los Angeles, which parlayed its near-monopoly in movie production, the attractions of its scenery and climate, and its access to oil, into a 133 percent population increase between 1920 and 1930. But most of these places, especially those on the edge of the continent, were cities of the future. To 1930, cities in the urban-industrial heartland still set the pace and direction of national economic growth, and in these cities, too, the forces that molded the characteristic form and structure of the early-twentieth-century city stood out most clearly. Now, as before, the gigantic industrial cities captured the eye and imagination of novelists and architects and stirred the deepest concern among the nation's most talented journalists.

None of the great industrial centers of the interior attracted more attention than Chicago, the "shock city" of the early twentieth century. Part of the Windy City's mystique derived from its extravagances. A ragged settlement of fifty people huddled on the prairie along the eastern shore of Lake Michigan in 1830, the city contained 3.3 million res-

125

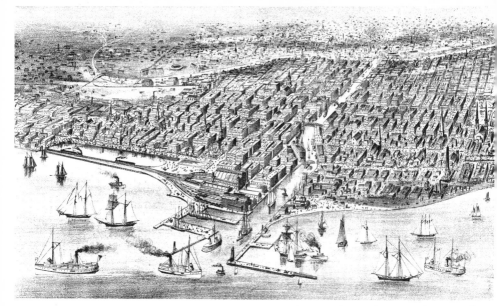

66   Chicago about 1870. South Water Street *(see preceding page)* is in the center foreground.

idents sprawled over more than 100 square miles a century later. But something more than rapid growth made Chicago special. It struck Lincoln Steffens at the turn of the century as "first in violence, deepest in dirt, loud, lawless, unlovely, ill-smelling, irreverent, new . . . the 'tough' among cities, a spectacle for the nation."[1] And in the view of many, then and since, Chicago also possessed the most resourceful social reformers, the most lively network of ethnic neighborhoods, the nation's most gifted civic designers. The newness of the city, its great size, and the inventiveness, daring, and diversity of those who built its social fabric and physical environment gave Chicago its national notoriety, and the history of early-twentieth-century Chicago illuminates the process that projected into the twentieth century the late-nineteenth-century tendency toward sprawl, center-periphery division, and the development of ethnic neighborhoods.

Residential Configuration

Immigrants and Blacks Immigrants and blacks, though seldom thought of as planners, played an important part in determining the direction of Chicago's growth. Although an alien society imposed severe constraints upon their range of options, they nonetheless made choices as they moved into the life of the city. Some of those choices pointed toward ethnic isolation for their groups and a pattern of cultural pluralism for the city, but the lure of the American dream dictated other decisions, which directed them toward a new culture, one neither entirely Wasp nor wholly pluralistic. The interaction of these separationist and integrationist impulses helped establish a pattern of intergroup relations that assured both the persistence of Chicago's patchwork quilt of ethnic neighborhoods and the tendency of the city to expand in area.

Chicago attracted a persistent flow and astonishing diversity of immigrants. After 1880 and into the 1900s, as before, Irish, Germans, and Scandinavians continued to come, but now they were outnumbered by southeastern Europeans—Italians, Russian Jews, Poles, Greeks, and

67 An 1883 advertizement for new homes aimed at Chicago's rapidly growing German immigrant population.

68   Workers' homes in late-nineteenth-century Chicago.

various peoples from what is now Yugoslavia. The foreign newcomers, initially as suspicious of one another as of native Americans, settled in distinct colonies near the central business district along Halstead and Maxwell Streets, Milwaukee Avenue, and in other nearby areas recently abandoned by the previous immigrants (from northern and western Europe) who, when they could afford it, began gradually to push toward the better housing and greener districts between the suburban fringe and the slums. Yet even in the new areas a significant degree of ethnic clustering persisted, although the density of concentrations by group in these outer wards did not match the high levels of inner-city neighborhoods, and borders constantly shifted as old settlers gave way to new. "But you could always tell," as columnist Mike Royko recently recalled, "which state you were in by the odors of the food stores and the open kitchen windows, the sound of the foreign or familiar language, and by whether a stranger hit you in the head with a rock."[2]

The increasing numbers of blacks abandoning Dixie for northern cities helped perpetuate the division of Chicago into "turfs" occupied by hostile groups. Between 1910 and 1930 the nonwhite population of Chicago jumped from 44,000 to 160,000. Though the blacks, too, settled into colonies, their residential experience differed sharply from that of white newcomers. Regardless of how successful or ambitious blacks were, white antipathy confined them within tightly segregated areas near the heart of the city. Most of them moved into the Near South Side and spread block by block in a southerly direction. By 1920 the great black ghetto there stretched from the edge of the central business district to Hyde Park and the University of Chicago, some six miles away.

Old Residents vs. New   Equally significant in determining Chicago's twentieth-century residential configuration was the broader conflict between old residents and new. At the time, Mr. Dooley, a fictional Irish bartender created by the brilliant Chicago humorist, Finley Peter Dunne, lampooned both the defensive reaction of the older residents, who in tribal panic asserted the presumed superiority of their presumed Anglo-Saxon heritage, and the organized enthusiasm of the newcomers, who just as eagerly sought to prove that they, too, fit into the city's cultural mainstream:

> Th' Bohemians an' the Pole Anglo-Saxons may be a little slow in wakin' up to what th' pa-pers calls our common hurtage, but ye may be sure they'll be all r-right whin they're called on. . . . I tell ye, whin th' Clan an' th' Sons of Sweden an' th' Banana Club an' th' Circle Francaize an' th' Pollacky Benivolent Society an' th' Rooshian Sons of Dinnymite an' th' Benny Brith an' th' Coffee Clutch . . . an' th' Turrnd'yemind an' th' Holland Society an' th' Afro-Americans an' th' other Anglo-Saxons begin fer to raise their Anglo-Saxon battlecry, it'll be all day with th' eight or nine people . . . that has th' misfortune iv not bein' brought up Anglo-Saxons.[3]

69   Maxwell Street in Chicago about 1906.

But the conflict between native Americans and "old" immigrants on one side and newcomers on the other was serious, and its residential dimensions both reflected and perpetuated the division of the city into a center-periphery pattern. The twentieth-century Ku Klux Klan, for example, drew its strength from lower-middle- and middle-class Americans in the nation's most dynamic metropolises. While the Invisible Empire's appeal to city dwellers stemmed from a variety of sources, neighborhood transitions provided one of the most fruitful. The uneasy feelings generated by this continuing process approached hysteria when ambitious and successful first- and second-generation "new" immigrants and blacks tried to move out of the old neighborhoods and buy or rent in the Zone of Emergence. In Chicago during the 1920s the Klan developed first in Englewood, Woodlawn, and Kenwood (neighborhoods that lay just beyond the growing South Side black ghetto), and drew disproportionate support from West and North Side communities, where the threat was ethnic rather than racial.

The response to the expansion of black neighborhoods was most violent. In late July, 1919, at the height of the movement of southern blacks

70 During race riots in 1919 a Chicago mob searches out a black man whom they later stoned to death.

into Chicago, race tensions erupted into a major riot. For months before the conflagration, whites bombed homes of blacks in marginal neighborhoods. Job competition contributed to white resentment, and many Democratic politicians credited GOP Mayor William Thompson's spring victory to the solid Republican vote in black precincts. On July 27 a black youth swimming in Lake Michigan on the South Side drifted across the "line" separating the white and black beaches. Whites threw stones; one found its target, and the boy sank and drowned. Soon fights broke out at another beach, and rumors of a black uprising spread into adjoining white neighborhoods. White mobs took to the streets, and race warfare broke out along the inner edge of the Zone of Emergence. A state investigating commission later credited much of the violence to white youths organized into tight-knit ethnic-flavored clubs such as Roger's Colts and the Hamburg Social and Athletic Club. In four days of fighting, 15 whites and 23 blacks died, 178 whites and 342 blacks suffered serious injuries, an estimated 1000 homes went up in flames, and property damage mounted into the millions of dollars. It was the worst race conflict in Chicago history, and as in previous such encounters in other places, whites initiated the violence and temporarily forgot their ethnic rivalries in a united racist attack on the blacks. The lengthy casualty list and the residential source of the confrontation underscored the new significance of territorial divisions as symbols of status and havens of security in the new city.

Exclusion   The strong sense of territoriality, however, was not the only obstacle faced by newcomers seeking access to better neighborhoods. The fluid economic and financial conditions of the late nineteenth century, which eased the assimilation and outward movement of "old" immigrants, was rapidly giving way to a more structured situation in which education had become a prerequisite for public as well as private employment. But even those with the diligence and good fortune to acquire the appropriate credentials often found their paths blocked, for "old" immigrants jealously guarded recently acquired occupations in both the public and private sectors, excluding newcomers in favor of their fellow Germans, Irish, or Scandanavians. In Chicago this placed the recent arrivals from southeastern Europe in a unique position. Entering a highly competitive society in which money and residential mobility stood as the chief measures of success, they found it increasingly difficult to rise by assiduous dedication to a legitimate occupation in trade, business, manufacturing, politics, or public service. Most, to be sure, managed to get along in this way. But others followed a different path.

Crime Crime provided many Chicago immigrants one entrance into the American way of life. In the 1890s and 1900s many recently arrived newcomers achieved some success by exploiting their fellows. Immigrant bankers, since they operated outside the regulations controlling the larger state and federal banks (and often acted as steamboat ticket agents and conducted other minor businesses as well), found lush opportunities to defraud. Other neighborhood entrepreneurs did just as well. Labor agents often fleeced ignorant immigrants desperate for a job, and quack doctors, shyster lawyers, and merchants who adulterated their wares provided needed goods and services while lining their pockets in the process. Recruits for these shady operations came from the neighborhood gangs, which, as they had for several generations of city dwellers, not only filled a social void but also frequently introduced young men to a culture in which petty fraud was regarded as "smart."

By a peculiar conjunction of circumstances organized crime as well as petty criminality became a major agent of Americanization for a small but notorious minority of Italians between 1900 and 1930. But Chicago's first "syndicate" was not run by Italians. From 1879 to 1890 Michael Cassius McDonald headed a highly effective coalition of criminals, politicians, and compliant policemen. After the assassination of Mayor Carter Harrison in 1893, however, McDonald's grip loosened and independent organizations appeared on the North, West, and South Sides of the city. In the Loop, "Hinky Dink" Kenna and "Bathhouse John" Coughlin, the masters of First Ward politics, also controlled gambling. They were deeply impressed by the way in which John Colosimo, an Italian immigrant and street sweeper, organized his fellow "white wings" and regularly delivered them for the Democratic ticket in the First Ward. As a reward, Kenna and Coughlin backed Colosimo for precinct captain. Thereafter he acquired a string of brothels and saloons, and then entered legitimate business by opening a restaurant that attracted Chicago's social elite and show celebrities. By 1914, Colo-

132

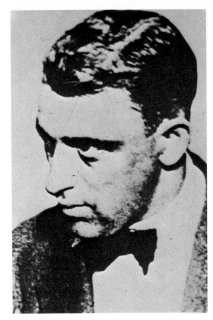

71 and 72 Two of Chicago's gang leaders—Mike McDonald *(left)* and Hymie Weiss *(right)*. McDonald was influential toward the end of the nineteenth century; Weiss' notoriety came in the 1920s, when his rivalry with Al Capone ended in his death.

simo and his aide, Johnny Torrio, ran a vice ring that ranked among the top three in Chicago and operated in the suburbs as well as in the city.

With the coming of national prohibition in the 1920s, Torrio, with his chief lieutenant, Alphonse Capone, engaged in bloody warfare— there were over 500 gangland murders during the decade—for control of the liquor business in Chicago. But the contest was not fought strictly along ethnic lines. The Torrio-Capone group contained Slavic, Jewish, and Irish elements. One of its chief competitors, the North Side Gang, was led by Barney Bertoche, Dion O'Banion, Hymie Weiss, and George "Bugs" Moran, and employed several Italians, including "Schemer" Drucci and the nine Aiello brothers. Indeed, by 1930, according to one careful study, Italian Americans constituted but 31 percent of the leadership in Chicago's organized crime, while 29 percent were Irish and 20 percent were Jewish. By that date, in short, Italian criminals in Chicago had dropped the Old World village provincialism that had led them to regard anyone from outside one's village—Italian or otherwise —as aliens. They also merged with other groups (excluding, like other

133

white Americans, the blacks) and, adopting American business techniques, centralized the chain of command in their criminal activities in order to compete more effectively in the quest for money. Organized crime in Chicago, like education and politics, was a popular way to realize the American dream of material success, and once sufficiently "Americanized," ethnic criminal entrepreneurs joined the trek from the old neighborhoods out to the edge of town.

Annexation The spectacular increase and diversification of Chicago's population and ethnic tensions and violence helped shape its neighborhood residential structure and ignite the explosion of the city's physical expansion, but politicians and business and professional leaders also played an important role. Late-nineteenth-century politicians, for example, abetted both the sorting out of people by economic class and ethnic origin and the city's expansive tendency by supporting a series of annexations, the largest of which occurred in June, 1889, when voters in a surrounding 120 square miles of territory elected to join the city. Annexation, in turn, encouraged the outward push of population and the creation of relatively homogeneous neighborhoods. It brought police and fire protection to places unable or too small to create their own forces, and it gave suburbanites access to the city's more efficient and cheaper water and sewer systems. Urban sprawl, in short, did not stem entirely from the operation of abstract economic and technological forces or the push of upwardly mobile people from poor neighborhoods; it also gained force from the decisions of office-holders and voters in all sections of the metropolis to make it official public policy.

Influential Individuals The decisions and inventiveness of individuals also played an important part in determining the city's specialized commercial and industrial land use pattern during the early twentieth century. Business and professional leaders, often working closely with politicians, exerted the major influence in this respect. They in effect decided that the centripetal-centrifugal pattern of business and industrial locations that first took shape in the late nineteenth century was most appropriate for the twentieth. Their choice assured the continued vitality of the central business district, dotted the expanding residential area with neighborhood shopping centers, and created new and scattered industrial districts both within and well beyond the city's limits.

Commercial and Industrial Aspects

The "Loop" Some of this group's most spectacular achievements were in the center of town. Between 1880 and 1900, Chicago architects and businessmen laid the foundation on which the city built a new skyline. By the late nineteenth century the continued development of the city's commercial and industrial capacity and the growth and outward thrust of its population placed an enormous premium on central sites for retail, office, and financial buildings. In the 1880s a real estate company and two Chicago architects, Daniel H. Burnham and John Welborn Root, combined their resources to relieve the pressure of soaring land values in the central business district. Their solution was to

73 The iron framework—an innovative construction technique of the time—of the Unity Building in Chicago in 1891.

utilize the space above the congested core, and they constructed the city's first two skyscrapers. The Montauk Block and the Monadnock Building, though only ten and sixteen stories high, respectively, overcame the difficulty of erecting massive edifices—the Monadnock required tapered walls 72 inches wide at their base—on Chicago's soft sand and clay by resting the structures on "floating foundations." More important, in 1887 William LeBaron Jenney designed the true progenitor of the modern skyscraper, eliminating the massive masonry of contemporary bearing-wall construction by using wrought iron and steel beams as a skeleton on which he hung the Home Insurance Building. Others soon followed suit, and the subsequent vertical growth of the city at its core permitted the central business district to retain its economic dominance.

Ribbon Developments   The Loop was not, however, the city's only growing commercial district. In response to the growing population in outlying residential neighborhoods, entrepreneurs built clusters of stores at intervals of about a mile. In more densely settled areas streets were lined by buildings with stores on their ground floors and, commonly, dwelling units in the upper stories. At the intersection of major arteries in these ribbon commercial developments, land values soared, and taller buildings and a greater variety of stores appeared. Farther out, larger regional shopping centers sprang up; they serviced broad areas containing thousands of inhabitants and rang up impressive sales figures. By 1930, Chicago had developed six of these in an arc several miles from the Loop. They contained not only the drugstores, specialty shops, variety stores, groceries, and saloons that catered to the impulse-buying habits of their patrons, but also several banks, at least one department store, and, in the 1920s, elaborately ornamented movie "palaces" capable of accommodating as many as 5000 at a time.

Residential and commercial sprawl, and the continued growth of Chicago as an industrial center, made manufacturing sites near both the heart of the city and working-class neighborhoods increasingly scarce. For a time the organized industrial district, an idea introduced into the United States by Chicagoans, seemed the best answer to the problem of finding factory sites close to workers and to supporting services. Under this scheme the organizers of the district assembled land in sparsely populated sections within the city, laid out streets, installed utilities, and often provided financial services, engineering and building consultants, and occasionally even dining facilities and clubs for executives. The first of these in-town industrial developments was organized in 1890 north of the Union Stock Yards on the South Fork of the South Branch of the Chicago River, and the Central Manufacturing District, as the organization was known, subsequently developed several other tracts.

Satellite Cities   Yet industry, too, was caught up in the centrifugal thrust. Manufacturers pinched by tightening congestion near the heart of town and by residential competition for the limited available space within the city sought expansion locations close to the city's labor supply, but far enough out to be roomy and cheap. The railroad and the telephone, the latter of which made it possible to coordinate the operation of several plants from one location and to make immediate contact with far-flung but related businesses, gave them access to a broad territory. Blue Island was one of the first places in the Chicago area to feel the impact of these technological innovations. Originally a commercial village sixteen miles south of Chicago, it was inundated with Chicago-based industries after the 1880s. By 1910, however, industrialists were moving even farther afield. The construction of the Chicago Outer Belt Line railroad in a broad arc 35 miles from the Loop paved the way for the rapid growth of Waukegan, Elgin, Aurora, Joliet, Chicago Heights, and Gary as industrial "satellite" cities within the orbit of Chicago.

PLANNING: THE SOCIAL FACTOR

These industrial projects and developments were motivated principally by economic and geographic considerations, as well as by the desire of boosters to have Chicago retain its rank as the nation's "second city" and perhaps even to push it into first place. But in these same years another effort to mold the physical form and structure of cities and to control their growth took shape; this one focused on social benefits. Specific strategies varied, but the diverse proponents of planning the physical development of American cities for social improvement were united by a common concern over the destructive influence they felt

137

74 and 75 Two forms of transportation in Chicago about 1886: Above, a car of a commuter's interurban line to the suburb of Blue Island; below, local trolley service in the city.

the continued expansion and flux of the cities had on the sense of community in urban America.

A group that concentrated on inner-city neighborhoods sought not only to secure recreational amenities, efficient public services, and decent housing for the slum districts, but also to create close social relations that would foster the development of a democracy in which all participated. They fought not only for the establishment of neighborhood parks and playgrounds and tenement reform, but also for the development of social centers to serve as focal points for the growth of a sense of community. In Chicago, as elsewhere, settlement houses and institutional churches spearheaded this drive. But groups in various cities invented special approaches that were then adopted in other places. In Rochester, the emphasis fell upon opening the public schools after traditional closing hours to all age groups for a variety of purposes, including the debate of civic and political issues; in Cincinnati, Wilbur C. Phillips organized 31 social units at the block level to help local residents take the lead in planning and improving local health care and in providing wholesome activities for the youth in the area.

Neighborhood builders scored some impressive successes, but the accomplishments of another wing of the planning movement were more dramatic, or at least more visible. Though its supporters, too, worried about slums, crumbling neighborhoods, the seemingly dwindling sense of community, and the fate of democracy in the new cities, they were as much concerned with providing for new growth as with improving and stabilizing older districts. Seeing the sprawling new urban centers, including the suburbs and satellite cities beyond the central city's corporate limits, as interdependent economic and social entities, they preferred to plan on a metropolitan basis, and they regarded the suburban thrust as the savior of the cities.

The roots of this movement went back to the mid-nineteenth century, when the advent of mass rapid transit intensified the rate of peripheral urban growth. Between 1860 and 1880, for example, New Orleans as well as several northern cities experimented with a metropolitan police force, and in subsequent years a host of towns across the country established metropolitan port and park authorities. But these were administrative adjustments designed more to accommodate, rather than en-

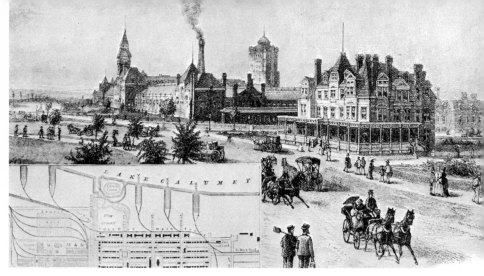

76 George Pullman's planned "model" suburb of Chicago about 1885. The inset (lower left) shows the plan of the city and its relation to the Pullman railroad car works.

courage, sprawl. After 1884, however, advocates of the metropolitan perspective adapted the approach of the neighborhood enthusiasts to create new communities on the edges of cities. Most of these planned suburbs, like the influential Country Club District at Kansas City, Missouri, were designed for affluent families only. But in Cincinnati a private philanthropist had Mariemont laid out as an ideal garden community for the respectable working class, and as early as the 1890s George Pullman constructed a planned industrial suburb south of Chicago that provided work, housing, and public and community services on the assumption that model physical facilities would produce a model community and model citizens.

The Grand Design: Daniel Burnham

Neither administrative adjustment by the creation of special metropolitan governing districts nor the new suburban community planners approached the comprehensive scale of metropolitan planning envisioned by Daniel Burnham's grand design for the development of Chicago. Convinced that "good citizenship is the prime object of good city planning," Burnham was the central figure in placing Chicago in the forefront of the metropolitan planning movement. Burnham served as chief architect of the Columbian Exposition, the World's Fair held in Chicago in 1893, and after that event he followed closely the various proposals to develop parks along the lake front on the South Side. Between 1906 and 1909, under the auspices of the Commercial Club, he superintended the development of the Plan of Chicago, ranked by some scholars as the single most influential city-planning document of modern times.

Distinguished by its determination to provide for the future growth of the city as well as to take account of immediate needs, Burnham's plan was bold, practical, flexible, and comprehensive. Its objectives were to assure the city's economic efficiency; to make it a comfortable, convenient, and esthetically pleasing place in which to live; and, above all, to encourage unity. Its method was, on the one hand, to establish a broad physical framework within which future improvements could be fit and, on the other, to propose specific projects for immediate implementation. But the plan recognized and accepted the basic facts of urban growth in the late nineteenth century. It did not propose to decen-

77   Caricature of city planner Daniel Burnham painted by Theodore Must about 1893.

tralize or fundamentally alter the central business district or its role in the metropolis, and it did not view urban sprawl as an evil. Indeed, the plan implicitly endorsed the metropolitan perspective and the conviction, widespread at the turn of the century, that continued geographic expansion, if balanced by the encouragement of institutions and physical facilities that emphasized unity and social integration, would provide the metropolis with the economic base, social coherence, and political stamina needed to retain its vitality.

The Six Points   The plan was composed of six main items; it urged: improvement of the lake front from Winnetka on the north to the Indiana state line on the south; creation of a highway system on the rim of the city; relocation of railway terminals and development of a complete freight and passenger traction system; acquisition of an outer park system and of parkway transport circuits; systematic arrangement of streets within the city to facilitate movement to and from the central business district; and lastly, promotion of centers of intellectual life and

78   A rendering of the Burnham Plan for redeveloping Chicago. The view looks east toward Lake Michigan from a proposed civic center.

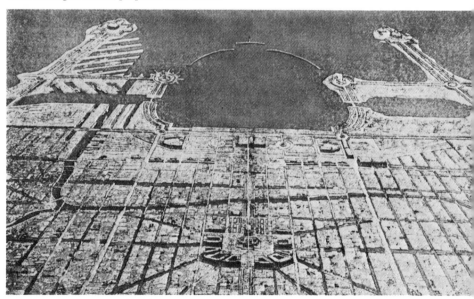

civic administration so related as to provide coherence and unity for the metropolis. In his presentation of the scheme Burnham closed with the modest surmise that if the plan were adopted it would "produce for us conditions in which business enterprises can be carried on with the utmost economy . . . while we and our children can enjoy and improve life as we cannot now do. Then our own people will become home-keepers, and the stranger will seek our gates."[4]

Chicago Plan Commission   The Commercial Club, though it raised $85,000 to draw up and publish the plan, recognized that it lacked the resources to make Burnham's vision a reality. Only the politicians and the voters could do that. Consequently, the selling of the plan began at once and became a permanent fixture in Chicago politics. The first task, the establishment of a nonpartisan Chicago Plan Commission, was turned over to Mayor Fred L. Busse, a Republican, the son of a German immigrant, and a bachelor who lived above the office of his coal company. He persuaded the city's "low-brow" aldermen not only to create the Commission and confirm the 353 citizens he recommended to man the agency, but also to approve a Democrat, Charles H. Wacker, as chairman.

Wacker was a felicitous choice. He was, as one contemporary described him, "first a brewer, then a building association man, wealthy but not too much so, loyal to German musical affairs, mixer in different sets, supporter of various things" and, most important, a resourceful publicist. He and other civic leaders saturated the city with information about and pleas to support the plan. They planted newspaper articles, mailed a booklet to voters, prepared a textbook for school children and had it placed in the public school curriculum, presented innumerable stereopticon lectures to clubs and associations, and even put together a two-reel promotional movie that played at Chicago theaters. As a result, voters repeatedly approved bond issues needed to finance the improvements and acquiesced to higher taxes as well. Despite the breadth and expense of many of the plan's ideas, many of the proposals had been carried out by 1930.

Yet pushing each project through was never easy. The widening of North Michigan Avenue above Randolph Street, and the construction of a new bridge across the Chicago River entailed the passage of a bond

143

issue, a court suit brought by those who declared the improvement a boon only to "rich automobile owners" and "the swells," and 8700 separate property settlements. Construction of South Wacker Drive and the removal of the South Water Street Market, the city's food distribution center, to a point two miles to the southwest produced a long contest with old occupants and ultimately required the compensation of 8000 displaced property owners.

The redemption of the lake front from commercial and industrial uses was perhaps the most sensational achievement of the planners. That undertaking, though not completed by 1930, involved acquiring millions of dollars of landfill to extend the shoreline into the lake, persuading the Illinois Central Railroad to electrify its trains into the city and to build a new terminal, convincing commercial interests to give up valuable developed and undeveloped sites, and then fighting off encroachments on the new land by those who sought to exploit it for economic gain. But the work persisted, and the sight of laborers along the shore became a routine part of the cityscape. Navy Pier, reaching 3000 feet into the water just east of the Loop and containing a dance hall, theater, recreational facilities, and a mass transit station as well as commercial installations, was finished by 1916. The passage in 1919 of the Lake Front Ordinance started reclamation of the scruffy shoreline south of the Loop. Beginning with Grant Park, the work created eight miles of parks and beaches, one island, and recreational facilities southward to Jackson Park, the site of the 1893 World's Fair. By 1930, improvement of the lake front to the north had built up a graceful and distinctive front yard of beach and park for the imposing string of exclusive high-rise apartments along the city's "Gold Coast."

The Plan of Chicago, and the generation that launched it, did not establish a Utopia on Lake Michigan. But the energy and persistence with which its supporters maneuvered the proposals through the controversy, bickering, and political roadblocks surrounding each phase of the work embodied the spirit, goals, and assumptions that characterized the urban renaissance of the first two decades of the twentieth century. "Make no little plans," wrote Daniel H. Burnham in 1912, "they have no magic to stir men's blood. Make big plans; aim high in hope and work. . . . Let your watchword be order and your beacon beauty."[5]

79 View north along a boulevard (now Michigan Avenue)
proposed in Burnham's Chicago
redevelopment plan.

But the backers of the Chicago Plan succeeded, in the final analysis, because of the plan's nonrevolutionary nature. Burnham, like the ethnics, blacks, annexationist politicians, commercial and industrial builders, and neighborhood planners, regarded congestion as a major evil of the turn-of-the-century city. Armed with a new transportation technology and buoyed by the surge of economic growth after 1900 they chose expansion, land use specialization, and decentralization. In the process they created an expansive city of shifting neighborhoods, which fulfilled the aspirations of neither the small- nor big-community advocates. Both groups failed because they agreed that inner-city districts could and should continue to function as staging grounds for mobility, and because both accepted the prevalent notion that a single-family house in a better neighborhood embodied the American dream. As a result, twentieth-century Chicago looked very much like late-nineteenth-century Chicago: It had a central business district surrounded by rings of successively more prosperous residential neighborhoods, pockmarked with shopping centers and industrial districts, and the whole was in a constant state of expansion, flux, and friction. But twentieth-century Chicago did not just grow; it was built that way.

Notes

[1] Lincoln Steffens, *The Shame of the Cities* (New York: Hill and Wang, 1963), p. 163.

[2] Mike Royko, *Boss: Richard J. Daley of Chicago* (New York: Signet, 1971), p. 31.

[3] "On the Anglo-Saxon," in *Mr. Dooley in Peace and War* (Boston: 1898), pp. 55–57.
[4] Daniel H. Burnham and Edward H. Bennett, *Plan of Chicago* (Chicago: The Commercial Club, 1908), p. 124.
[5] Quoted in Miller, *Boss Cox's Cincinnati*, p. xi.

Bibliography

Bell, Daniel. *The End of Ideology*. New York: The Free Press, 1960. Contains a chapter discussing crime as a ladder of social mobility in the twentieth century.

Condit, Carl W. *The Chicago School of Architecture*. Chicago: Univ. of Chicago Press, 1964. Discusses the late-nineteenth- and early-twentieth-century burst of architectural creativity associated with Chicago.

Buder, Stanley. *Pullman: An Experiment in Industrial Order and Community Planning, 1880–1930*. New York: Oxford Univ. Press, 1967. An important and critical study of the Pullman experiment.

Jackson, Kenneth T. *The Ku Klux Klan in the City, 1915–1930*. New York: Oxford Univ. Press, 1967. Analyzes the rise and decline of the Klan in cities across the country and challenges the traditional view of the Invisible Empire as a rural reaction against urbanization.

Lubove, Roy. *The Urban Community: Housing and Planning in the Progressive Era*. Englewood Cliffs, N.J.: Prentice-Hall, 1967. Kindly disposed toward the regional planners, the author presents a lucid account of their views. He sees conservation, housing codes, city planning, park development, the "city beautiful" movement, and the Garden City idea as attempts by a new set of professional experts to wrest control of urban land use policy from business interests.

Mayer, Harold M. and Richard C. Wade. *Chicago: The Growth of a Metropolis*. Chicago: Univ. of Chicago Press, 1969. Contains the best analysis and exposition of the growth of early-twentieth-century Chicago, including a succinct and perceptive account of the conception, promotion, and implementation of the Burnham plan.

Nelli, Humbert. *Italians in Chicago, 1880–1930: A Study in Ethnic Mobility*. New York: Oxford Univ. Press, 1970. A sympathetic study, free of nostalgia for the old neighborhood. It emphasizes the instability, transiency, and assimilation of the Italian immigrant community.

Schmitt, Peter J. *Back to Nature: The Arcadian Myth in Urban America*. New York: Oxford Univ. Press, 1969. Maps out an important segment of the intellectual context within which professional planning and the modern city grew.

Scott, Mellier Goodin. *American City Planning Since 1890*. Berkeley: The Univ. of California Press, 1969. The most comprehensive treatment of the modern American city-planning tradition.

Spear, Allan H. *Black Chicago: The Making of a Negro Ghetto, 1890–1920*. Chicago: Univ. of Chicago Press, 1967. Read with Nelli's book on Italians, this volume suggests some of the differences between the experience of foreign immigrants and that of "indelible immigrants."

Tuttle, William M., Jr. *Race Riot: Chicago in the Red Summer of 1919*. New York: Atheneum, 1970. An analysis of the 1919 Chicago riot that reaches, as the title indicates, well beyond the city limits for the sources of the conflict, but gives due account to the residential dimension.

The Roaring Twenties, 6
the Depression, and
the New Deal

Though most historians treat the 1920s and 1930s as separate units, it is appropriate from the urban perspective to handle them as one. In the first place, the incidence of group violence in this twenty-year span declined abruptly. The spreading influence of voluntary associations, the organization of factory work forces into small groups, and the spatial separation of disparate population elements, which increasingly characterized the modern city in the early decades of the twentieth century, functioned as pacifying influences on urban society. Despite the ethnic tensions of the 1920s and economic troubles of the 1930s, city dwellers on the whole responded with a discipline and restraint that contrasted sharply to the riotous tumult associated with similar circumstances in the mid- and late nineteenth and early twentieth

80   Residents of Harlem march in 1924. The decorous demonstration is in support of the rights of colored peoples.

centuries. Instead of taking to the streets, dissatisfied individuals and groups now more often registered their discontent peacefully, strove for improvement through pressure group tactics, and worked out conflicts through compromise. The development of this more disciplined urban population also helps explain the emergence of the Democratic Party as the party of the big cities after 1924 and as the majority party in the 1930s, for even under conditions of great stress, coalition politics now appealed more strongly than did factional strife or political violence and revolution.

Finally, the 1920s and 1930s can be considered as one unit because the new Democratic urban coalition supported an administration that adopted a national urban policy based upon an extremely pessimistic analysis of metropolitan problems. First articulated in the 1920s, that analysis suggested that only massive action could save the cities, and its proponents gained access to the president and his advisors in the 1930s. As a consequence, for the first time in the history of the modern city, the initiative in directing the growth of cities passed from the local to the federal level.

THE PEACEFUL CITIES

Those who felt American urban society seemed about to come apart in the second quarter of the twentieth century could point to numerous ominous signs. During the 1920s Wasps and grandchildren of "old" immigrants in the cities indulged themselves in the wave of super-patriotism and intolerance that produced a revival of the Ku Klux Klan, a stubborn attempt to enforce prohibition, and federal legislation designed to stop the influx of "new" immigrants. At the same time a variety of ethnic spokesmen attacked the melting-pot ideal. Most, like Horace Kallen, preferred a culturally plural society in which the identity of minority groups would be preserved, but Marcus Garvey, the black nationalist leader who established the United Negro Improvement Association, advocated a return to Africa for his proletarian followers among the "indelible immigrants" trapped in the central-city ghettos. Despite the outburst of tribalism among native born, immigrants, and blacks, however, and even during the crushing hardships of the Great Depression, the cities remained surprisingly peaceful. Be-

81 Marcus Garvey, exponent of the return-to-Africa alternative for America's blacks.

tween the mid-1920s, when ethnic tensions were at their peak, and 1932, when the economy hit rock bottom, neither ethnic mobs nor bread rioters took over the streets of the nation's major urban centers. Though the cities had serious troubles in these years, the incidence of group violence declined to well below the level it had reached in the nineteenth century.

Influence of Volunteer Agencies

The proliferation and growing influence of voluntary organizations —themselves originally a reaction to the novelty, broadened spatial scale, and disorder of life in the emerging modern city—played an important role in restraining extremist behavior. In the Zone of Emergence the building and loan associations, neighborhood improvement groups, mutual-benefit associations, and organizations of butchers, grocers, and realtors, and other special-interest groups all served not only as buffers against economic insecurity but as bases of sociability and arenas of education into the life style of the region as well. They fostered increasing use of the arts of persuasion and negotiation, inhibited the old tendency to resort to force, and deterred mob action. Though slum dwellers, as in the late nineteenth century, fared less well at organizing and sustaining these kinds of groups themselves, they often received a helping hand from Zone residents, and suburban residents continued to support settlement houses, churches, and other agencies of acculturation in the central city. But political machines still played the more critical role in organizing the inner city and in channeling the frustrations of slum life into peaceful outlets.

Industrialization Factors

The relationships that grew out of the structure of work organization in corporation-dominated society also helped reduce the pressures of urban life. In large-scale industrial organizations a new elite of management experts consciously arranged production processes so that the total work force was divided into relatively stable cells of five or so individuals responsible to a supervisor or foreman. The cell functioned as a kind of on-the-job family. The foreman channeled to the group the daily flow of information needed by the workers and entered into a daily and personal give and take with its members. Veterans of a group taught new members the tricks of the process and helped establish a general consensus on the pace of work, punctuality, and codes of behavior. But the influence of the work group as an agency of social control reached beyond the plant gate and office building entrance. Among his peers within the cell the worker found friendship, informal education on a limitless range of subjects, and a sense of belonging. In these ways the cellular arrangement of work cushioned the workers against both the impersonality of the large bureaucracy and the frustrations, problems, and ethnic and other resentments that the worker brought with him to the job. Thus, this group organization of work added, in Sam B. Warner Jr.'s phrase, another "lattice of loyalties" to the complex forces of social control in the city.

The hierarchical structure of big business organizations also limited psychological tensions among workers. Above each work group, regardless of its place in the bureaucracy, always stood a higher group, relieving those below of the burden of responsibility for task decisions and for determining such matters as hours and wages, vacations, and layoffs. Compared to the mid-nineteenth-century city work structure of isolated artisans, semiskilled workers in three-man shops, or unskilled laborers moving from job to job, the urban employee of the 1920s and 1930s labored in the relative social and psychological security of the group hierarchy within the bureaucracy. These strengthened work associations within large institutions enhanced the ability of the metropolis to absorb conflict and variety, and at the same time conditioned workers to and reinforced the tendency to seek group outlets and negotiated solutions for grievances both inside and outside the shop.

Warner has also pointed to other characteristics of cities—particularly those experiencing relatively slow rates of population growth— that helped reduce the incidence of group violence in the 1920s and 1930s. One of these was the residential pattern by which the poor, the unskilled, the blacks, and most of the foreign-born occupied the oldest and cheapest housing in segregated neighborhoods near the heart of the city, which tended to separate the groups from one another and from those of the more prosperous, with which they might otherwise conflict. With the restriction of immigration in the mid-1920s and the ces-

82   The automobile brings increased mobility (and traffic problems) to Americans: St. Louis in the 1920s.

sation of significant rural-to-urban migration in the 1930s, neighborhood transition in the central city and the expansion of slum districts slackened, reducing further the potential for clashes between inner-city groups and along the boundaries between slums and the Zone of Emergence.

Residential Segregation

Increasing uniformity and greater security of neighborhoods beyond the slums also tended to reduce the combustibility of big cities in the 1920s and 1930s. The twentieth-century working- and middle-class family enjoyed a margin of spatial freedom that gave them a measure of relief from the tedium, tensions, and restraints of job routine. The grow-

152

ing prevalence of automobile ownership enabled large numbers of people to take their leisure in widely dispersed locations across the metropolis among people essentially like themselves. But neighborhood atmosphere was equally important. Home ownership, which brought with it a larger degree of privacy and a reduction of tension within the household, ran high generally beyond the slums, and because of the generally similar cost of housing in given residential districts, broad areas on the periphery tended to be made up of people of similar income and class status. As a result, children could run free in relative safety, and the process of socialization proceeded peacefully outside the household under the supervision of the school, the church, and the neighborhood. Here, too, adults could live informally without the pressure of having to display their status by outward signs of dress and demeanor. On the periphery as in the center, then, metropolitanites of the 1920s and 1930s lived in fairly well-defined neighborhoods among people like themselves. Seldom in their daily activities did they meet strangers who posed a threat to their values, attitudes, or sense of place and continuity. Thus, the spatial separation of cultural groups and socioeconomic classes limited the opportunities for violent conflict in the modern city.

THE NEW DEAL

The same factors that inhibited violent confrontations between antipathetic groups in the cities also assisted skillful politicians in discouraging extremist political reactions among those dissatisfied with their condition of life. Even during the worst times in these years, discontented individuals registered their protest through coalition politics, not through revolution or stubborn and massive adherence to special-interest factionalism. This tendency manifested itself at all levels in the political system, but its most dramatic expression occurred in national politics. In the middle of the Depression decade, incredibly diverse groups of urban voters, including those whom the social, economic, and political system had discriminated against well before 1929, cast their ballots for a Democratic presidential candidate who aimed not to destroy "the system," but merely to remedy its defects. Indeed, Franklin D. Roosevelt and the New Deal proved so appealing that the Democrats

153

managed to bridge the gaps among ethnic groups and between the center and periphery of the city. The willingness of these heterogeneous voter blocs to unite behind a "middle-way" program rested in large measure upon the stabilizing social and psychological cushions provided by spatial segregation, the influence of voluntary associations, and the group organization of work. Because of that cushion even the most disadvantaged segments of the urban electorate were tolerant enough to settle for the compromises inherent in coalition politics and secure enough to prefer reform to revolution. But political stability in the 1930s also depended upon the Democrats' ability to offer the right candidate and the appropriate program at the right time.

The general outline of the new coalition first took shape in 1932. That year the Democrats elected Franklin D. Roosevelt, only their second president in 42 years, and took the House of Representatives with a majority of 190 seats. In 1934, instead of losing House seats, the Democrats added ten more to their total, and in 1936 they re-elected FDR by an overwhelming majority. Though the spatial, social, and economic organization of the city and the impact of the Depression help explain the revival of the Democrats, domestic and international migration and coincidence also played an important role.

83 Franklin D. Roosevelt during the first of his four terms as President.

84 A deserted Ellis Island in 1928, after the major waves of immigration had subsided.

As Samuel Lubell has noted, population shifts in the early twentieth century cleared the path for the Democrats. Not only had the majority of the American people become urban between 1910 and 1930, but a sizable proportion of city dwellers was made up of the foreign-born (see Ch. 5, p. 126ff.) and inclined to raise large families. As early as 1910 a majority of children in the schools of 37 of the nation's largest cities had foreign-born fathers, and in places like Duluth, New York, and Chicago two out of every three school children had immigrant parents. The First World War and immigration restriction in the 1920s cut off the flow from Europe, but it was replaced by a stream of whites from the Appalachian hills and of blacks from the rural South. Between 1920 and 1930 over 6.5 million individuals left the farms and hills below the Ohio and 4.5 million of them went to New York, Chicago, Detroit, and Los Angeles. The domestic migrants arrived in the cities just as the mass of second-generation immigrants became adults and entered political life, and all of these groups suffered sharply during the early years of the Depression.

85 Al Smith during his campaign for President in 1928.

But the revolution in national politics began before 1929, and it started in the cities. Throughout the 1920s Republican pluralities in the large industrial centers dropped steadily. In 1920 the GOP counted 1,638,000 more votes than the Democrats in the nation's twelve largest cities. That margin dropped in the three-way race of 1924, and in 1928 it was transformed into a Democratic plurality of 38,000. It was Al Smith, not Franklin D. Roosevelt, who initiated the revolution in the urban vote.

A closer analysis of the returns indicates that Smith's support in the cities ran strongest among those of foreign stock. Since the turn of the century the resentment of immigrants against those on top smoldered as a factor in national politics. Either the newcomers did not turn out in significant numbers for national elections, or they followed the lead of Republican machines in one city and Democratic machines in another. None of the presidents after 1900 managed to strike the spark of vicarious identification among the new immigrants. But by the late 1920s the public schools and other agencies of education raised the level of political sophistication among the urban foreign-born and their children. And in 1928 the Democrats nominated Al Smith of New York for president. Smith came from a lower-class, Catholic, New York City family. He wore a brown derby and spoke in a raspy East Side accent, and his career in New York politics showed that he could be loyal to the boys in Tammany Hall and still take progressive stands on social and economic questions. Though he hoped to keep religion out of the campaign, others did not, and the resulting cleavage seemed to pit the prosperous native-born Protestants against the poor and predominantly Catholic underdogs.

The returns for 1928 verified Smith's appeal to big-city immigrants. He carried seven of the nineteen major cities that had a preponderance of immigrant stock, although in 1920 all nineteen had voted Republican. More significantly, in each of those nineteen cities, whether carried by Smith or not, the Democratic vote rose dramatically. In none of them was the increase less than 100 percent, and in several of those that Smith carried, the Republican vote dropped from that of 1920. None of the major cities dominated by native white voters showed much of an increase in either the total vote or the vote for Smith.

These figures suggest, then, that Smith first galvanized the urban foreign-stock vote into a potent Democratic force. The market crash and subsequent economic slump reinforced the immigrant-Democratic connection and added to the coalition large numbers of "forgotten" voters from the middle classes who suffered as the Depression deepened between 1930 and 1932. It was in 1936, however, that the Democrats' urban strength peaked. In that election, only Maine and Vermont went Republican, and the Democratic plurality in the twelve largest cities soared from 1,791,000 in 1932 to 3,479,000. The results read the same in smaller cities as well, regardless of regional location; the size of the foreign-born, native, Catholic, Protestant, black, or Appalachian population; or whether the town had a union tradition or an open-shop heritage. While the "Smith revolution" and the Depression virtually assured Roosevelt the victory in 1932, the 1936 landslide represented a ratification of Roosevelt's policies during the latter years of his first term.

In retrospect, 1935 seems to have been the year of decision. By that time the worst of the Depression had passed, and as conditions slowly improved, the willingness of voters to follow just any strong voice

86 A New York department store during a "Dollar Day" sale, one of many futile merchandising schemes aimed at reversing Depression trends.

flagged and the critical spirit revived. In 1935 the gradual pace of economic recovery and the unpopularity of some of the early New Deal programs—the once popular NRA (National Recovery Administration) was now derisively tagged the National-Run-Around—threatened to erode Roosevelt's support among the urban lower-middle and middle classes. At the same time, critics such as Francis Townshend and Huey Long wooed the poor and the elderly with share-the-wealth programs, while on the right Detroit's famous radio priest, Father Charles Coughlin, gathered strength among the masses of poverty-stricken city dwellers who struggled to subsist on meager relief checks. For Roosevelt and the nation the major question now became whether to commit the federal government to a continuing role in controlling the national economy and providing broad programs for social welfare, or to return to the old formula of merely regulating the competition of organized economic interests and letting the wealth "trickle down" to the rugged individualists below.

Federal Aid and Intervention

In 1935 the New Deal took new directions. That year the president and his advisors pushed through Congress the Wagner Labor Relations Act, which pleased workers; a "soak the rich" tax, which delivered a small but politically significant measure of relief for both the lower-middle and the middle classes; a Social Security Law, which reassured the elderly and appealed to younger people who could not expect to lay up a nest egg for their old age; and a measure that established the WPA (Works Progress Administration), which provided jobs for the unemployed. These measures, plus the Public Utilities Holding Act, which struck at those FDR dubbed "economic royalists," undercut Townshend, Coughlin, and Long and rested upon the assumption that most urban Americans approved of federal experimentation in controlling the economy and in providing broad programs for social welfare. The administration had measured the mood of the electorate correctly, for others in 1935 also opted for a new order. That year witnessed the formation of the CIO (Committee for Industrial Organization), the spearhead of the drive to establish industrial unions, which for the first time brought immigrants and their children, white Appalachians, and blacks together into one labor organization. And, in the wake of a New York City race riot, Harlem shopkeepers hired black employees, Mayor Fiorella La Guardia appointed the first black magistrate, and Tammany Hall named its first black district leader. These events indicated the willingness of many to strike out on new paths, and the massive Roosevelt victory of 1936 demonstrated a similar commitment among even more. In a variety of ways those who had received the fewest benefits from urban life in the first third of the twentieth century received their initial recognition between 1928 and 1936, and the election of 1936 became, in a sense, a referendum on the new directions expressed in the Al Smith and Roosevelt revolutions. The strength of the Democratic Party in the cities after 1928 lay in its ability to activate and coalesce elements that, since 1880, had been fragmented, mutually hostile, and indifferent to national politics. The Democrats became the majority party by unifying the disparate groups in the central city and allying them with the periphery to form an unbeatable reform coalition.

87   A "Hooverville" in New York City in 1932. The shacks were occupied by unemployed and their families.

The Roosevelt revolution in politics also brought the cities and the federal government into a closer relationship. Municipal officials made the first move in that direction shortly after 1929. During the first two years of the Depression, 58 mayors, the editor of *American Cities,* and the national organization of city managers all urged Congress to help meet the unemployment crisis. President Hoover responded by urging the cities to meet their responsibilities to the jobless with local resources and by selecting a week in October of 1931 for a concerted Community Chest drive in 174 cities to raise money for relief. Though most cities exceeded their quotas, the effort failed to raise enough funds to meet the rising needs.

Mushrooming unemployment rolls generated a growing sense of despair in cities across the country. By 1932 New York had one million out of work, Chicago 660,000, and places like Toledo and Akron listed over 50 percent of their work force as unemployed. Private charitable agencies were swamped, and declining land values coupled with rising tax delinquencies crippled municipal and state efforts to take up the slack. Virtually every city developed a "Hooverville" of makeshift shanties, and in New York a drained reservoir in Central Park was transformed into a temporary residential community known as "Hoover Valley." On the edge of the cities "aborted suburbs," their fire plugs, sidewalks, and empty lots engulfed in weeds, stood as uncompleted monuments to the blasted dreams of those who had looked to pleasant homes on the cool green rim of the metropolis. The bad times bred a pervasive despair and frustration summed up in the story of the man who enquired after a hotel room. "For sleeping or jumping?" responded the clerk. The promise of the city had turned into a bad joke.

Desperate municipal officials and city-based politicans kept the pressure on Washington for aid. Roosevelt, whose election stemmed from strong support in central-city districts and the adjacent wards where conditions were worse, delivered. The New Deal's banking, social security, and labor legislation as well as its alphabet soup of relief agencies and work programs—FERA, WPA, PWA, NYA—helped ease the strain of unemployment and economic disruption across a wide spectrum of the urban population. As the Democratic urban coalition broadened, so, too, did the New Deal's aid to the cities. By the mid-1930s federal intervention touched on almost every aspect of municipal policy. One count in 1936 revealed 500 points of contact between the federal bureaucracy and the cities in the fields of planning, zoning, education, health, internal improvements, relief, and housing.

A National Urban Policy

Some critics have scored the New Deal's reaction to depression in the cities as a hodge-podge of piecemeal responses aimed at resolving specific problems rather than at developing a systematic program to provide

88 Street-widening about 1935, one of many diverse projects of the WPA—the Works Progress Administration, a New Deal agency that provided jobs for some of the unemployed.

for balanced urban growth. Yet, viewed in another light, a pattern emerges that suggests that the New Deal's myriad ties to the cities did in fact represent the emergence of the country's first national urban policy. Because of the nature of the New Deal's urban coalition, however, the policy had two parts. One responded to Roosevelt's boss constituency, for like the favorite local programs of machine leaders it answered to the immediate needs of people without agonizing over root causes of problems or the more remote social consequences of solutions. The other part, which appealed to the "reformers," rested upon an abstract analysis that stressed the organic interdependence of the elements in metropolitan life and sought to benefit the whole. The New Deal's urban policy responded to both the center and the periphery.

Reviving the Suburban Trend

The boss aspect of the New Deal's urban policy received the lion's share of the funds. It assumed that the turn-of-the-century process of urbanization was basically sound and needed only to be stimulated and coupled to a continuing policy of annexation to restore the cities to their earlier vitality. Based on a commitment to perpetuate the outward expansion of the metropolises, this policy laid the foundation for the emergence of the automobile, the truck, and the bus as the principal means of rapid transit in American cities. High on FDR's list of emergency measures to relieve unemployment stood highway construction, particularly highways leading into and out of the great cities. Adding local and state funds to federal dollars, local authorities not only expanded the highway mileage in their areas but also devised the cloverleaf traffic exchange, created the limited-access and divided super highway, and constructed motor bridges, like the eight-mile San Francisco–Oakland Bay bridge, which tied central cities to a broader territory. These transport innovations made substantial changes in the face of the metropolis without disturbing the established outline. Until the 1930s suburban real estate development clustered about the streetcar and railroad lines. Now the highways and the internal combustion engine freed the commuter from the constraints of the rail, and gradually the interstices between the old radial lines of settlement began to fill.

89 New York "Mortgage Marchers," unable to meet home mortgage payments during the Depression, appeal to President Roosevelt for help.

90 In Longview, Washington, in 1935, one of the sixty families moves into its new home in a federally subsidized homestead project. The cow (plus chickens, fruit trees, and two acres of land) came with each house.

The revival of the residential suburban trend was spurred by New Deal home financing and labor legislation. The establishment in 1933 of the Federal Housing Administration (FHA) dramatically reduced the cost of home construction. The homeowner, in return for the payment of a small annual fee, received a mortgage guaranted by the FHA. With that backing, lending agencies were willing to reduce their interest rates to 4 percent and to issue loans that extended over a period of 25 years, a sharp contrast to the 6 or 7 percent, 5-year loans and second mortgages common in the 1920s. At the same time labor legislation that reduced the working week from 60 to 40 hours permitted a mass of blue- and white-collar Americans to join the ranks of the commuters and to have leisure time on weekends to devote to their families and to home improvements. And, as the working-force migration toward the periphery mounted, the earlier drift of factories toward the urban fringe revived. Even retail facilities, including branches of downtown department stores, now joined the suburban trend.

Slum Clearance

The New Deal also sought to do something about the slums. However, instead of providing the poor with a minimum income high enough to enable them to obtain FHA loans and join the suburban trek, the federal government stimulated slum clearance and the construction of low-rent yet modern apartments in the heart of the city. Beginning in 1934, under the public works program, a few sections of the nation's most festering slums were demolished and replaced with public housing, and in 1937 the United States Housing Authority was created by the federal government to subsidize local housing efforts. Though this program did not begin to meet the needs of the poor for decent shelter, these measures reflected the administration's commitment to decentralize the metropolises. Both FHA and public-housing programs assumed that after economic recovery the inner city would continue to function as a staging ground for mobility—that an improved physical environment within the slums would help the poor to earn their way up the socioeconomic ladder and out into the more pleasant neighborhoods.

91 Lewis Mumford, one of the early planners who saw in the city's physical structure the origins of its social ills.

"Urbanologists" and Decentralization

The other aspect of the New Deal's urban policy drew upon a starkly pessimistic analysis of metropolitan growth. The optimism about the possibility of creating an orderly and cohesive society within the framework of the great metropolises, which buoyed Daniel Burnham and other municipal reformers and city planners of the early twentieth century, receded after 1920. During the "roaring twenties," regional planners, such as Lewis Mumford and Clarence Stein, and academic specialists in urban studies, such as Louis Wirth of the "Chicago school" of sociologists, formulated a biting critique of the modern American metropolis. Influenced in part by the notion that the passing of the frontier endangered democracy in America and by the new nostalgia for a more compact city built closer to the human scale, the first generation of professional "urbanologists" implied that poverty, inequality, dependency, insanity, delinquency, and crime found their natural home in the city, and that the continuing concentration of a growing proportion of the total population in sprawling metropolises had pro-

165

duced a supermaterialistic and hollow society. More grimly still, the indictment contended that any social organization as large, densely settled, heterogeneous, and mobile as the twentieth-century big city must either experience periodic episodes of widespread disorder or have depersonalization and the disorientation of uprootedness level off its people into a dull and mediocre mass susceptible in times of stress to the appeals of demagogic totalitarians of the extreme right or left.

The remedy struck a vital nerve, for it borrowed from and played upon the longing for the lost rural frontier, the new nostalgia for small communities, and the contemporary movement to the suburbs. It stressed the need to counter sprawl by creating, around the great centers, a ring of settlements that would offer the best of both rural and big-city life, and it stressed also the necessity of encouraging balanced rural-urban development in the desolate countryside through programs of rural "electrification, improved soil management and farming, and general regional rehabilitation." But the special emphasis fell on the advantages of life in the outlying towns. Here excess population from the crowded metropolises and the depressed countryside could live in small "many sided, balanced, self-maintaining" communities, "fully equipped for industry, business, social life, and culture . . . linked together with the central metropolis in a new kind of urban pattern." The advantages seemed overwhelming, for the concept merged the ideals of the old metropolitan and neighborhood planners of the early twentieth century and provided for the redistribution of the population and the preservation of country life. The new pattern, in Mumford's words, "would permanently preserve the countryside for farming and recreation and bring together the neighborhood, the city, and the metropolis in a new constellation . . . called the regional city."[1]

Model Suburbs and New Towns   The New Deal never made a wholesale commitment to regional unity, but it approached it with several tentative thrusts. One of the most dramatic came when the Resettlement Administration decided to establish a series of model suburbs. Rexford Guy Tugwell, the director of the agency, was well aware of the spectacular and disorderly growth on the periphery of the cities during the 1920s and felt the country needed 3000 of the planned communities if the outward thrust were to be successfully disciplined. In fact, however,

92 Greenbelt, Maryland, one of the government's Depression-era planned communities at the time of its completion (1937) at a cost of $15 million.

only three—one each on the edge of Milwaukee, Cincinnati, and Washington, D.C.—were built. Based upon the "garden city" idea, a notion popular in both England and the United States that Mumford built into the regional-city concept, these places were intended to do two things: provide low-income urbanites with a chance to escape the inner city, to live and work in an environment that combined the best aspects of country and city life; and create markets for the marginal farmers living in the rural-urban fringes of the great metropolises. Though none of the three communities fully lived up to these expectations, they represented, as one student has put it, "the most daring, original, and ambitious experiments in public housing in the history of the United States."

But the New Deal's national urban policy, in its attempt to decentralize the population, went beyond the concept of the "green belt" encircling an urban center. FDR, as Tugwell once noted, felt rural life superior to urban, and much of the New Deal reform program aimed at redistributing the population. To lure urbanites closer to nature, for instance, both the Federal Emergency Relief Administration (FERA) and the National Industrial Recovery Act (NIRA) provided for the establishment of new towns. Those under FERA can be construed simply as relief measures, but the NIRA set up 100 communities, most of them rural farm settlements, specifically designed to provide urbanites with havens from vulgar industrial society. Ironically, those close to major cities soon assumed the characteristics of suburban subdivisions and, in that form, survived the 1930s. As for the rest, once the worst of the early Depression had passed, their inhabitants scurried back to the cities.

The TVA   The Tennessee Valley Authority (TVA) also fit within the administration's population decentralization and redistribution scheme, and Mumford and the regionalists "exulted" at how closely it approximated their ideals. The most ambitious single social-planning venture undertaken by the New Deal, the TVA, promoted economic development in a lagging region without massive urbanization by coordinating the construction of hydroelectric dams, the promotion of farming and of agriculture-oriented industries, and the conservation of forest, land, and water. By most criteria it worked out well, though one representative of the older city planning condemned it for "representing planning as a Davy Crockett–coonskin-cap retreat from life." In any event, TVA, like NIRA's Homestead Division and, in a sense, the green-belt towns, expressed the twentieth-century suspicion of the modern city, the desire to deconcentrate and redistribute the metropolitan population, and the impulse to reverse the farm-to-city flow and afford more people the chance to live in an environment that more equitably balanced nature, agriculture, and industry.

Old Patterns Persist

Taken as a whole, however, and judged by its accomplishments, the federal response to depression in the cities was conservative. The New

Deal's urban policy neither envisaged nor produced a radical transformation of metropolitan form and structure. The improvement of intrametropolitan transportation, the provision of low-interest loans for home construction, the effort to upgrade the housing of inner-city inhabitants, and the creation of garden city suburbs all fit neatly into the pattern of sprawling growth in and around cities that had developed after 1880. With the exception of TVA, the population redistribution and decentralization programs either collapsed or failed to attract enough support to assure their expansion or continuation, and the older, pre–New Deal patterns of rural-urban migration and suburbanization persisted into the 1940s. So, too, did the new pessimism about the urban prospect and the urban problems catalogued in the 1937 National Resources Committee report on the condition of cities. The Committee's list of metropolitan shortcomings included inadequate educational and recreation systems, chronic health hazards, the extreme and inefficient dispersal of population, duplication of administrations, sagging public services, ineffective planning and zoning, and a fragile economic structure easily "thrown out of gear and demoralized." Yet the new pessimism exaggerated the magnitude of the crisis and grossly underestimated the resiliency of the metropolises. Within a decade after the Second World War, boosters across the country were talking excitedly about the achievements of the mid-century "urban renaissance."

Notes

[1] Lewis Mumford, "The Frustration of Urban Planning," in Raymond A. Mohl and Neil Betten, eds., *Urban America in Historical Perspective* (New York: Weybright and Talley, 1970), p. 393.

Bibliography

Arnold, Joseph L. *The New Deal in the Suburbs: A History of the Greenbelt Town Program, 1935–1954.* Columbus: Ohio State Univ. Press, 1971. A lucid analysis of the greenbelt town experiment, which links the suburban projects to the New Deal program to "make America over" by striking a balance among rural, suburban, and urban life.

Conkin, Paul. *Tomorrow a New World: The New Deal Community Program.* Ithaca, N.Y.: Cornell Univ. Press, 1959. Provides a brief critical survey of New Deal efforts to build urban communities.

Gans, Herbert J. "Urbanism and Suburbanism as Ways of Life: A Re-evaluation of Definitions," in Arnold Rose, ed., *Human Behavior and Social Processes.* Boston:

Houghton Mifflin, 1962. A critical view of Wirth's seminal essay, which describes more recent approaches to the nature of metropolitan life.

Leuchtenburg, William E. *Franklin D. Roosevelt and the New Deal, 1932–1940.* New York: Harper, 1963. The best single-volume analysis of F. D. R. and the New Deal.

Lubell, Samuel. *The Future of American Politics.* New York: Harper, 1965. Perhaps the most readable account of the (Al) Smith and (Franklin) Roosevelt revolutions, and this edition brings the Democratic coalition into the 1960s.

Lubove, Roy. *Community Planning in the 1920's: The Contributions of the Regional Planning Association of America.* Pittsburgh: The Univ. of Pittsburgh Press, 1964. The best study of the assumptions and programs of the Stein, Mumford group.

McKelvey, Blake. *The Emergence of Metropolitan America, 1915–1966.* New Brunswick, N.J.: Rutgers Univ. Press, 1968. Contains useful information on the New Deal and the cities and on federal-municipal relations.

Wirth, Louis. "Urbanism as a Way of Life," *The American Journal of Sociology,* XLIV (1938), 1–24. The classic sociological statement of the "pathology" approach to the study of the city.

part three

RENEWAL
AND
CRISIS

The Postindustrial 7
Metropolis and the
Second Urban Renaissance,
1945–1960

The initiative for guiding the direction of metropolitan growth and improving the quality of urban life shifted, in the postwar era, from the federal government back to the local level. Several factors account for this devolution. The failure of New Deal policies to alter significantly the pattern of metropolitan growth drained some enthusiasm for federal leadership, and the general affluence of the postwar period dissipated the crisis atmosphere, which motivated federal intervention in the 1930s. In addition, because Republican control of the White House in the 1950s was less dependent on support from the big cities, urban problems were ranked as second- or third-priority items in the national budget. At the same time, renewed rural migration to cities and rapid outward expansion of metropolises revived the turn-of-the-century optimism about the natural vitality of American cities. In a period of growth and prosperity, city problems appeared amenable to local control and not due to any fundamental flaw in the configuration of cities and metropolitan areas or to basic weaknesses in American society. This was especially the case when most metropolitan leaders now ascribed their difficulties merely to a backlog of economic and physical problems stemming from the financial stringency of the Depression and the diversion of energy and funds to the war effort. In this context massive infusions of federal aid and the development of a national urban policy simply did not seem necessary. As a result, the second urban renaissance of the twentieth century, like the first, drew its vitality and direction from local leaders.

While the postwar metropolitan reformers chalked up some impressive successes, they failed to eliminate poverty and discrimination and other related problems outlined in the 1937 National Resources Committee report. In some places the new reformers lacked funds to do all that they felt necessary. But their failure derived in the final analysis from their inability to respond appropriately to new conditions. Their local perspective made it difficult for them to recognize the changing complexion of local problems—in turn, caused by changes in the larger society. They sought to renew their cities and, by implication, an older pattern of urban growth that they regarded as essentially sound. Their optimism led them to revive the strategies and goals of urban planners in the Burnham period, not to adjust metropolitan growth to peculiar local and national conditions as a new period in the urbanization process began.

THE RISE OF SERVICE AND FOOTLOOSE INDUSTRY

By the mid-twentieth century, American urban history had entered a new phase, one associated with the movement of society from the industrial into the postindustrial stage. Though the latter term can be misleading, it connoted a stage of growth in which technological advances reduced the proportion of workers required in the familiar producers' and consumers' goods industries and created new industries. Increasingly after 1945, the "service" sector of the economy assumed a

174

93 A concentration of footloose industry—primarily electronics—along Route 128 in the Cambridge, Massachusetts, area.

new importance in the employment structure, for now a larger proportion of the work force than ever earned its living in medium- and high-skill services such as retailing, dry-cleaning, hairstyling, and the law, medicine, education, and government. The new industries, such as the electronic, chemical, aircraft, aerospace, defense, and research and development firms, possessed two important identifying characteristics. They were "footloose" because they did not have to locate near their sources of raw materials, and they required a well-educated work force strong in management, information, and technological and scientific skills that took long training to acquire. These became the high-income and high-profit industries that produced a rapid rate of growth in the cities where they accumulated.

Effect on National Urban Pattern

As in earlier eras of significant economic changes, the shift in the economy affected the continental pattern of urban growth. The rise of the service sector and footloose industries placed a premium on locations well endowed with climatic, visual, and recreational advantages. Both push and pull factors accounted for this: First, the well-educated and generally affluent employees in the new growth enterprises pre-

175

ferred these kinds of residential amenities; second, the nature of the new industries and of the sophisticated air transportation and electronic communications networks freed manufacturers of the industrial era from the old necessity to choose locations in or near the urban-industrial heartland. Educational and high- and low-brow entertainment factors also proved important in the new locational competition, but additional universities, schools, orchestras, and sports arenas could be built into a pleasant environment relatively rapidly. The net result of the interplay of these forces between 1945 and 1960 made for rapid urban growth around the rim of the continent, especially in the states of Florida, Texas, Arizona, California, and in the older metropolitan areas of the northeastern seaboard. Though most of the major centers of the heartland also attracted some service and footloose industries, they managed merely to maintain a growth rate roughly equal to the national average, while the metropolises on the rim far outstripped that pace.

Intracity Effects

The emergence of the postindustrial economy had a lesser yet significant influence on the interior structure of metropolitan areas. The bulk of the footloose industries, and large numbers of the new service firms and agencies, selected suburban sites. There the managers and technicians could find residential neighborhoods with views, slopes, high ground, fresh air, and open space, and from these outlying homesites they could readily drive to nearby recreational and entertainment districts and to the diversity of leisure activities available downtown. Indeed, by 1960, the outlying high-income neighborhoods had become dense enough that many entertainment entrepreneurs, including both restaurant and big-league baseball owners, began to move their facilities to suburban locations in order to provide easier accessibility for their major market. Lower-status groups, because they could not compete successfully for superior residential spots and because their lower incomes forced them to stay close to places of employment, had little choice except to follow the more gradual expansion of jobs in heavy and related industries out along the major axes of transportation, usually in low-lying and crowded valleys. In short, the postwar shift in

176

94 and 95   Part of Los Angeles showing Wilshire Boulevard and Beverly Drive, the major diagonal roads in the foreground, in 1922 *(above)* and in 1968 *(below)*.

96   Offices of the Pepsi-Cola Company (formerly in New York City) in the surburb of Purchase, New York.

the economy perpetuated the old tendency of the modern city to spread out and to disperse occupational opportunities over broad areas.

The metropolises also continued to accumulate an ever larger proportion of the nation's total population. To be sure, the core cities of metropolises seldom showed dramatic gains, but only a handful, like Scranton, Pennsylvania, or Lowell, Massachusetts, lost population in the 1940s or experienced losses severe enough to pull their metropolitan population down in both 1950 and 1960. Most places surged upward. The number of metropolitan areas containing one million or more people increased from 11 in 1940 to 23 in 1960; the percentage of the total population living in major metropolitan areas moved up from 57 to 63; and the urban proportion of the total population rose to 64 percent in 1950 and to 70 percent in 1960.

The postwar metropolitan population explosion caught some experts by surprise, for demographers in 1940 had expected relief from urban population pressure in the future. The long decline in the rate of population growth due to natural increase—associated with modernizing, industrializing, and urbanizing societies—had already begun in the United States at the time of the first federal census in 1790. This tendency, though veiled by the massive infusion of immigrants, continued through the nineteenth and twentieth centuries, and the rate reached its lowest point in the great Depression of the 1930s. Viewed from the vantage point of 1940 the history of the American population indicated a continuation of the long-range trend toward slow rates of population growth by natural increase and a slackening in the pace of urban growth. However, post-1940 affluence and patterns of economic growth combined with the impact of the Second World War and the Korean conflict produced a reproduction generation of generally affluent, highly educated persons clustered in professional and growth industry occupations who married early and increased their rate of childbearing. After 1940 the level of natural increase soon bounced back up to the mark of the early twentieth century.

Despite the reproductive prowess of the mid-twentieth-century urban generation, not all of metropolitan growth between 1940 and 1960 can be attributed to natural increase. Internal rural-to-urban migration, stifled during the Depression years, revived after 1940. In that decade it increased at the rate of 1.3 million persons a year, and in the 1950s it dropped only slightly to about one million per year. Northern cities, as they had before 1930, attracted large numbers from the South, including almost 1.5 million blacks. They, like migrating white southerners, settled in central-city slum districts, where both groups competed for space and jobs with smaller numbers of Chicanos and Indians. A surge of movement out of Puerto Rico, which reached 40,000 in 1946, peaked at 70,000 in 1953, and persisted at lower yet substantial levels thereafter, contributed to the enduring ethnic diversity of the slums.

At first glance the trek of poor whites and nonwhite newcomers to northern cities seemed to make economic sense. According to a 1957 article in *Fortune* magazine, the inner city remained crowded during the affluent fifties because "there are jobs to be had," for the newcomers could find employment opportunities as "sweepers at General Motors . . . scrap throwers at Inland Steel . . . handtruck pushers around New York's garment center." In fact, however, the postindustrial metropolis worked a cruel hoax on recently arrived migrants. A large share of them followed traditional migratory paths to the urban-industrial heartland, not to the locus of the most rapid economic growth on the rim of the continent. The best opportunities in every metropolis, moreover, now occurred in the outlying fringe, not in the center of the city. By the late 1950s, matters were made worse by several factors—factory automation, a sluggish economy, declining consumer demand, and conservative federal fiscal policies. In this context the postwar migrants into the cities faced difficulties that matched, if they did not exceed, those confronting other groups that, in the past, had sought opportunity in the nation's urban centers. The new arrivals faced the indignities and hardships of poverty, discrimination, unemployment, and poor housing, and many had to live with the hidden hunger of malnutrition as well. By 1960 more people in the United States lived in the broken-down houses and tenements of the slums than on the farm, yet they remained "invisible" until an awakened social conscience, aroused in part by books like Michael Harrington's *The Other America* (1963), stirred a new concern in Washington for the elimination of poverty.

97 Entitled "Room with a View," a 1949 cartoon comments on postwar housing shortages.

Room with a View—from *The Herblock Book* (Beacon Press, 1952)

Critics of federal policy contended that the national government let the cities down in other ways between 1945 and 1960. Both the Depression and the Second World War deferred improvements in the urban physical environment, and in the late 1940s federal officials promised much but delivered little that was new. The Civil Aeronautics Act of 1946 empowered its administrator to advance grants-in-aid to public agencies that measured up to federal standards in airport maintenance and planning, but failed to provide adequate safeguards against the enormous potential for tawdry residential and commercial sprawl implied in planting the major interurban transportation facilities of the future on the edges of the nation's metropolises. In 1947 Congress established the foundation for a national network of highways, a program (expanded in the 1950s) that provided for miles of roadways in and around the metropolises as well as for interurban connections. Commuter expressways speeded metropolitan decentralization without improving the inner city and absorbed massive sums of federal revenues that might better have gone toward resolving urban problems of higher priority.

98 Housing "starts" (units begun) for selected years during the period 1925 to 1946. The data are from a report to the President and Congress made in 1946.

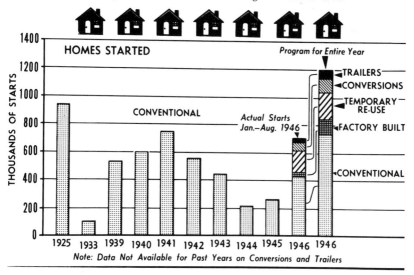

99 One measure taken to relieve the postwar housing shortage: quonset huts used for residences in Rhode Island.

Appropriately placed and imaginatively designed housing for a variety of income groups surely ranked as one of those high-priority items, but it was 1949 before Congress moved to enact appropriate legislation. Title I of that year's Housing Act provided for the construction of 500,000 low-rent dwellings over a four-year span and appropriated $500 million to aid cities in undertaking urban redevelopment projects. Yet these programs failed to relieve the housing problem. City planners regarded the $250 million per year annual housing allotment as paltry, private capital responded less enthusiastically than expected, and in 1956 only $13.5 million had been drawn for projects. Schools, recreation and sanitation facilities, and pollution control also received some federal dollars, but Fiorello La Guardia's complaint in the late 1940s best summarized the assessment of the federal effort by most big-city spokesmen: "We ask for bricks and stones and plumbing," grumbled the Little Flower, "and they give us mimeographed press releases."[1]

LEADERSHIP: "NEW BREED" MAYORS

Clearly the most energetic leadership in urban affairs after the war came from the metropolitan, not the federal level. It came, moreover, without substantial changes in the structure of local governments. The early-twentieth-century wave of enthusiasm for city manager and commission forms of municipal organization persisted but proved most popular in suburbs and smaller, homogeneous cities. The prospect of federalized metropolitan governments, like that which encompassed Miami and Dade County, Florida, attracted more attention than adoptions. Most of the other major metropolises, like Philadelphia, either developed or retained the strong mayor-council system.

The men who occupied city hall took on no easy task. Hemmed in by a ring of jealous suburban governments and hampered by the activities of independent authorities over which they had no control, they struggled to meet growing demands for services as best they could with revenues that chronically fell short of needs. Yet most observers in the postwar period agreed that the big-city mayors provided a quality of leadership equal to that in any other era of the nation's history.

The "new breed" mayors of the 1950s came from no common mold and worked in a variety of local frameworks. Raymond Tucker had been an engineering professor before taking control in St. Louis, and Frank P. Zeidler of Milwaukee also had a professorial background. DeLessups Morrison of New Orleans came to power in a revolt of insurgents against an entrenched organization and then used old-line political methods to put his program across and turn his loose following into a tight-knit organization. Richard J. Daley of Chicago differed from all these. He came up through the regular organization and proved a competent administrator and astute political operator despite his humble origins and frequent rhetorical fumbling. "We will go on," he once promised an audience at the University of Chicago, "to a new high platitude of success."

Though they came from a variety of social and economic backgrounds and functioned in diverse milieus, the men who provided new strength in city hall had some characteristics in common. Typically they held a college degree, usually in business or law, and had reached middle age before taking office. They worked long hours six and sometimes seven days a week, devoted a large share of their time to press conferences, to television and radio reports to the voters, and to getting out press releases on their accomplishments. They also spent four or five evenings

183

a week at banquets, policy meetings, gatherings of neighborhood groups, and in negotiating strike settlements. Though most were Democrats, they conferred a great deal with city business leaders. Most of them also doubtless agreed with Mayor Daley's maxim that "good government is good politics," but like him they scarcely fit the stereotype of the "nonpolitical" leader.

This combination of attributes, but especially their sense of realism, their commitment to detail and getting things done, enabled new-breed mayors to spark and guide the twentieth century's second urban renaissance. They surrounded themselves with bright young men and put together vigorous and effective political coalitions determined to direct the economic and physical growth of their cities and to improve the quality of the environment. It turned out to be old stuff. The strategies for putting programs across, the substantial emphasis of the programs, and the kind of metropolis envisioned by the leaders of the renaissance looked and sounded remarkably like Burnham's plan for Chicago. Like federal officials, moreover, the metropolitan leaders of the mid-twentieth-century urban renaissance failed to recognize that newcomers to the cities had been trapped in poverty by the peculiar form of metropolitan growth in a postindustrial society.

MID-CENTURY PLANNING AND REFORM: PITTSBURGH

Nowhere did the accomplishments of the mid-century metropolitan reformers seem more astonishing than in the cities of the urban-industrial heartland, which had economies dominated by heavy industry. The experience in one of these—Pittsburgh—nicely illustrates the strengths, successes, and shortcomings of the twentieth century's second great burst of locally inspired metropolitan planning and reconstruction.

Pittsburgh had never been a lovely city. A strong center of manufacturing from the beginning, its smoke earned it the sobriquet of the "Black City" in the mid-nineteenth century. In 1900 it was, in many respects, a typical metropolis of the urban-industrial heartland. Here, as in other cities with a heavy manufacturing base, the era of Big Business gave the city an industrial sector characterized by efficiency, cen-

100   Workers' homes with steel mills in the background in Pittsburgh in 1909.

tralization, and long-range planning, and a physical appearance that, as Lincoln Steffens put it, "looked like hell, literally." Despite the efforts of a vigorous band of reformers after the turn of the century, conditions failed to improve. In the 1930s, Pittsburgh still presented, according to one of its most severe critics, a "scene so dreadfully hideous, so intolerably bleak and forlorn that it reduced the whole aspirations of man to a macabre and depressing joke. . . ."[2]

The city's economic prospects were no better. Indeed, as early as 1920, Pittsburgh had entered a long period of economic decline. Immense sums of capital and labor were tied up in a few large industries and unavailable for the launching of new and more rapidly growing industries. Because of its specialization in types of industry with very large plants and very large capitalization, the city had a notably small complement and variety of the kinds of supporting services upon which small and new firms particularly depend. Specialization, which had made Pittsburgh a boom city in the late nineteenth century, threatened

185

it with stagnation in the twentieth. The rate of population growth in both the city and the county declined after 1910, and during the 1920s unemployment ranged between 5 and 10 percent of the labor force.

At the same time, suburbanization and heightened traffic congestion in the central business district, a problem intensified by the increasing numbers of autos, trucks, and buses on the streets after the First World War, threatened not only to strangle the economy of the city and its region, but also to smother its ability to provide services and solve new problems. Congestion at the center coupled with the outward push of more prosperous residents (and of industries) reduced real estate values and limited the revenues that could be obtained from real property taxes. Annexation had been the traditional response to this dilemma. But in Pittsburgh, as elsewhere, opposition to annexation intensified after 1920, and during the next two decades the city and its suburbs remained deadlocked over the issue.

In 1939 the Pittsburgh Regional Planning Association decided to attack these interrelated problems, but the severity of the crisis had not generated new thinking. During the Depression years virtually everyone placed economic recovery at the top of the list of urban priorities. Given the traditional role of the central business district as the symbol and driving force of metropolitan prosperity, it seemed self-evident that urban revitalization could not be expected if the core business district continued to deteriorate. Like Daniel Burnham, the Pittsburgh planners assumed that urban poverty, inadequate housing, and other metropolitan problems could not be corrected until after the central business district had been revived. Consequently, the Association hired Robert Moses, the builder-planner-administrator who had proved so adept at channeling federal funds into New York City, and urged him to design a plan to restore the vitality of Pittsburgh's central business district, a triangle of land formed by the juncture of the Allegheny and Monongahela Rivers. Moses proposed a plan to clear the area of railway yards, develop a park at the point of the triangle, create additional parking space, institute flood and smoke controls, and construct a road system that would allow through traffic to bypass the central business district. The plan was received with a remarkably favorable consensus among business and professional leaders, but the war effort absorbed virtually the entire resources and energies of the city and deferred action on the plan.

Pittsburgh entered the postwar years with a declining tax base, a shrinking population, a metropolitan economy that had been stagnating since 1920, and a central business district choking in smoke, liable to disastrous floods, and strangling with traffic congestion. But in 1946 a bipartisan civic coalition emerged that commanded the finances, technical skills, flexibility, and political ingenuity to undertake an unprecedented and massive program of urban renewal. Because of the coalition's composition it was able to overcome the geographic, class, ethnic, and political divisions that had inhibited effective action in the past. Its leaders blurred the distinction between public and private activities, secured the cooperation of city, county, state, and federal governments, and merged the policies of the Democratic and Republican parties. The major difference between it and the group that engineered Chicago's plan in the early twentieth century was that in the former the critical leadership came from the politicians, not the business community.

101   The Pittsburgh Triangle in 1947, before redevelopment.

The key figure in the Pittsburgh "renaissance" was David L. Lawrence, the boss of the city-county Democratic machine and the most powerful Democrat in the state. Elected mayor in the fall of 1945, he served for a decade and a half, and in that period established himself as one of the new breed of postwar mayors. Though he saw his chief task as "the limited, tedious, persevering work of making things happen," Lawrence, like his contemporary counterpart in Chicago, Mayor Daley, was willing to listen to a wide variety of advisors, including Republicans, big business interests, and suburbanites.

The Allegheny Conference on Community Development

Before making the race for City Hall, Lawrence consulted with Mayor Fiorello La Guardia of New York, who told him he was "a God-damned fool" for seeking the office and turned him over to Robert Moses, who in turn urged him to work with Wallace Richards, director of the Pittsburgh Regional Planning Association. Richards had been a newspaper reporter and art critic, a public-relations man, and, in the mid-1930s, had supervised the planning of Greenbelt, Maryland, one of the New Deal's three model planned communities. After coming to Pittsburgh, he had, among other things, played an influential part in establishing, in 1943, the Allegheny Conference on Community Development (ACCD), a nonpartisan civic organization for research and planning on a metropolitan scale.

Coalition: The ACCD and the Democratic Machine The prime mover in the ACCD was Richard King Mellon, chief financier, industrialist, and businessman in the Pittsburgh region, whose interests reached into Gulf Oil, Alcoa, Westinghouse Air Brake, the Pennsylvania Railroad, Pittsburgh Plate Glass, and Pittsburgh Consolidation Coal. He was also a major contributor to the state GOP, and his legal counsel, Arthur Van Buskirk, chaired Allegheny County's Republican Finance Committee. With the support of Mellon, as Lawrence later pointed out, it was difficult for "every defender of private enterprise," including the Republican-dominated state legislature, to condemn as "socialism gone rampant" the establishment by a Democratic city administration of a public parking authority or the use of law to take

102 Groundbreaking cere-
mony during the Pitts-
burgh redevelopment pro-
gram. Mayor Lawrence holds
the shovel.

private property from one set of owners and sell it to another for development.

The ACCD, chaired after the war by John J. Kane, a political col-
league of Lawrence's and a county commissioner, proved to be a very
effective instrument. Working closely with other planning agencies,
it sponsored concrete and specific plans drawn by a variety of specialists
from a broad range of fields. In addition, it consulted closely with the
press and with voluntary and public agencies (both Richards and Van
Buskirk held public offices—on the Parking Authority and the Redevelopment Authority, respectively—as well as serving on the ACCD).
In this way the ACCD avoided public controversy and identified its
programs with the community interest, and its Republican connections
tied it to both central business district interests and suburban GOP
political strength.

The coupling of ACCD with the city Democratic machine completed
the renaissance coalition. That alliance broke into public view in 1945
during the Pittsburgh mayoralty campaign. By that time Van Buskirk
and the ACCD had persuaded the Republican state administration to
build a park at the point of the triangle and to construct a limited-
access highway to link downtown with the Pittsburgh airport. These

189

projects were announced during the mayoralty race as a means of bolstering the chances of the GOP candidate. But Lawrence, even though he had been a working Democrat since age 14 and had been raised in the "hate Mellon" tradition, announced that the park and highway projects represented the kind of state commitment for which Democrats had worked and would continue to work. Early the next year, as mayor, Lawrence moved to cement his ties to the GOP leadership by securing, in advance, bipartisan support for a state legislative package of eight bills to benefit the Pittsburgh region in such diverse areas as county smoke control, public parking, mass transit, waste disposal, and suburban-subdivision planning.

Pollution Control The coalition first demonstrated its effectiveness in the fight against air pollution, a problem that had long been a premier concern of environmental reformers and city boosters in Pittsburgh. The groundwork was laid in 1941, when the city's health di-

103 The Pittsburgh Triangle (see page 187) after redevelopment.

104   Dramatizing Pittsburgh's air pollution in 1947. The scene was staged by the Allegheny Conference.

rector took the lead in fighting for a strong antismoke ordinance. The Civic Club, Allegheny County Medical Society, and the League of Women Voters all endorsed the idea, and the Pittsburgh press gave the campaign full coverage. Simultaneously, the city Smoke Commission developed and publicized a persuasive set of arguments linking smoke to pneumonia, sinus ailments, lung damage, the destruction of vegetation, high cleaning bills, and the city's dirty image and inability to develop a diversified and dynamic economy. Out of the agitation came a strong ordinance requiring industry, railroads, commercial buildings, and residential consumers to use smokeless fuel or to install devices that limited the emission of smoke. Enforcement was to be delayed until after the war.

In 1946 Lawrence decided to enforce the law vigorously and to broaden its impact by making smoke control a county as well as a city responsibility. After securing the support of the city council, Lawrence turned to the ACCD. That body helped persuade both coal companies and the soft-coal miners not to fight the enforcement program and joined in the effort to secure a county ordinance. Mellon and the head of United States Steel put pressure on the Pennsylvania Railroad to call off its lobbyists in Harrisburg, who were obstructing the passage of state enabling legislation providing for county smoke control, and the ACCD

191

helped organize a grass-roots movement in the county that assisted Commissioner Kane in persuading his fellow commissioners to enact an ordinance.

But the most important battle in the antismoke campaign and the effort to launch the movement for a new Pittsburgh remained to be fought. The opposition now centered in lower-middle-income city wards, and in putting it down Lawrence demonstrated the importance of the machine to the civic coalition. In 1949, Lawrence faced a Democratic primary, and his opponent, Councilman Edward J. Leonard, sought to oust the dominating figure in the renaissance by raising the smoke issue. Enforcement of the ordinance had not been easy. There was seldom enough smokeless coal available for the huge Pittsburgh market, improvised mixes of bituminous and anthracite were often inefficient, high-priced, and difficult to ignite, and stokers were expensive both to install and to maintain. As Lawrence recalled it, "inspections, explanations, complaints, and troubles came in by the thousands."[3]

Leonard, who headed the Plasterer's Union and claimed powerful allies in the Building Trades and AFL Central Labor Union, sought to exploit the general dissatisfaction with the enforcement of the program among those whom Lawrence called the "Little Joes." Leonard argued

105 and 106 Before *(facing page)* and after *(right)* the smoke control program went into effect in Pittsburgh. The scene is at the Liberty Bridge and Tunnel.

that lower-income people often had to purchase coal a bushel at a time and frequently lacked bins for the storage of coal to feed the stokers even when they could afford the equipment and the purchase of coal in bulk. He also claimed that the "Little Joes" footed the bill for the changes while the big interests received privileged treatment in the city's enforcement program. Charging that Lawrence had become too friendly with Mellon and indifferent to labor, Leonard made a strong showing in the primary. When the votes were in he carried many of the predominantly labor wards, but Lawrence's aggressive campaign and the effective work of the regular Democratic organization in the remaining districts gave the mayor a narrow 27,000-vote majority. In the subsequent general election the Republican candidate adopted Leonard's strategy, but went down by 56,000 votes.

Economic Redevelopment   Meanwhile the coalition began to move on its massive program to revitalize the central business district. This phase of the movement began with the development of Gateway Center near the tip of the triangle. A 1945 statute gave the city the right to set up a five-man Urban Redevelopment Authority, which could condemn private property and resell it for development with private funds. This procedure had been used during the 1930s to provide low-cost housing,   193 but Pittsburgh stood among the first to use the power of eminent domain for economic redevelopment.

Lawrence appointed himself chairman of the Authority, and the agency, after convincing the Equitable Life Assurance Society that federal help would eliminate the flood threat in the triangle, induced the company to construct three large office buildings in the blighted area adjacent to the Point Park site. In the 1950s the state, the International Business Machines Company, and Bell Telephone put up office buildings; the Hilton chain constructed a hotel; and a local developer added a luxury high-rise apartment to the complex. After that, renewal activities in the central business district quickened. By the mid-1960s 25 percent of the triangle's 330 acres had been cleared and 60 major new structures had gone up, including a multipurpose civic auditorium and arena. By that time, too, other improvements, such as a river-front sports stadium, were in the planning stages.

Economic redevelopment projects soon scattered across the face of the city. Some of these permitted existing industries like Jones & Laughlin Steel to expand and modernize their plants; others provided space for commercial and residential as well as industrial development; and still others enabled the city's two universities, the University of Pittsburgh and Duquesne University, to expand and to broaden their educational programs. By the mid-1960s the city's renewal projects encompassed 1500 acres and involved a total public cost of $171.5 million, including $112 million of federal funds.

The economic-redevelopment projects were designed to hold industries and office headquarters about to abandon the city, improve the environment so as to attract new firms, make the city more competitive in the interurban struggle to secure convention business, and shore up the municipal tax base. But the coalition also intended to revitalize and diversify the regional economy by luring a broad variety of growth industries, particularly space, electronics, and research and development enterprises, into the area. The chosen instrument for the achievement of these goals was not the public authority, but the private development company. In 1955 a new agency, the Regional Industrial Development Corporation, was established and the following year it reported on prospective sites in a nine-county district. By 1966 the Corporation's Industrial Development Fund had $9 million of commitments to small, growing industries and was acquiring and improving sites for industrial packages and industrial parks.

Housing Renewal Given the structure of the civic coalition that guided the renaissance it is not surprising that top priority went to economic recovery. Though the renaissance had a social dimension, it rested on the old assumption that improved housing alone would somehow enable the poor to shed their poverty. To be sure, the clearance of blighted areas involved the elimination of incredibly dilapidated slums, both in the inner city and in the outlying industrial sections. Yet many of the renewal projects actually complicated the city's already desperate housing situation. The clearing of the Lower Hill district for the civic auditorium, for example, displaced almost 8000 of the city's poorest and most disadvantaged citizens, left them to find shelter in deteriorating and poverty-stricken neighborhoods, and did nothing to provide them with the skills and transportation necessary to get decent jobs in the service- and research-related industries. Worse still, the plans of the Regional Industrial Development Corporation envisaged the uprooting of 18,000 other low-income families.

The coalition responded by establishing ACTION-Housing, Inc., an agency that merged the old housing reformers with the new business and professional leaders in the renaissance coalition. The organization's immediate concern was not with providing for the desperately poor, but rather with the "forgotten third"—those families in the $4,000 to $7,000 income bracket that earned too much to qualify them for public housing. To meet their needs ACTION-Housing procured $2 million from private sources as a low-interest capital fund to lure builders into the low-income housing market. The program rested on the assumption that poorer residents could either find space in the city's 7000 federally sponsored public-housing units or move into the abandoned dwellings of the "forgotten third." Neither the assumption nor the program worked out. Private industry proved as inept as ever at constructing low-cost housing, and the number of poor families seeking cheap dwellings, augmented by the influx of blacks moving north after the Second World War, as well as by those displaced by renewal activities, proved more than public housing could accommodate. As a result the old slums and ghettos were torn down only to re-emerge in other sections of the city. The coincidence of these developments raised the pace of neighborhood change and the clash of cultures to levels approaching that common in the early-twentieth-century metropolises and intensified the flight to the suburbs.

Achievement: Limited

By 1960 it was not only clear that the social achievements of the renaissance had been limited, but doubts about its economic impact had also developed. During the 1959–1960 national recession the unemployment rate soared to 9 percent, and the federal government officially classified the region as a depressed area. Conditions improved in the early 1960s, but a 1964 survey concluded that the region's economic base had not changed substantially since the Second World War and added that prospects for new growth and diversification remained uncertain. Worse still, between 1947 and 1960, aggregate employment in twelve of sixteen basic local industries declined by 76,617 jobs, population figures revealed a sizable outmigration in the 20–29 age bracket, and a special federal census in 1965 discovered that the metropolitan area had suffered an absolute population decline over the preceding five years. The civic coalition's economic planning effort, though massive, was not of sufficient magnitude to counteract the national shifts in economic structure and urban growth, which worked to the detriment of the heavy-industry cities of the heartland.

107 Single-family housing development in a suburb of Pittsburgh.

Observers seeking a balanced assessment of the renaissance reached mixed conclusions. Pittsburgh in 1965 was a cleaner, healthier, and more exciting city than a generation before, and without the renaissance it may well have become an abandoned mill town. Yet the evidence clearly indicated that the regional economy was still dominated by heavy industry—stagnant and quite sensitive to fluctuations in the national economic cycle. The forces that directed the new growth industries to cities on the edge of the continent proved too strong to be overcome by the efforts of reformers in one area, and the failure of this aspect of the coalition's plan suggested that effective metropolitan planning in the postindustrial society would have to be federally coordinated. Yet in 1965 the more than 212 metropolitan areas continued the old urban imperialist tradition, each of them in its own way pursuing economic growth instead of controlling growth and concentrating on improving those functions that its population, economic structure, and regional location enabled it to perform best.

The social dimension of the Pittsburgh civic coalition's planning effort also failed. The inability of the renaissance to resolve the housing problem and growing protests about the persistence of poverty, the bitter mocking of urban renewal as "Negro removal," and the rising agitation for neighborhood conservation and citizen participation in the decision-making process suggested that the coalition and the traditional approach to metropolitan improvement had reached the limits of their effectiveness. Since cities on the rim of the continent as well as others in the interior experienced similar difficulties, it seemed patent that they, like Pittsburgh, had reached a critical stage in their development.

The planning tradition that clearly predominated in the 1940s and 1950s was that articulated in Pittsburgh, where essential policy decisions occurred at the metropolitan level and received uncritical sanction and assistance from federal authorities. The renaissance leaders placed top priority on massive central business district and industrial development programs designed to promote economic growth while merely meeting the subsistence needs of the poor. By 1960 this twentieth-century comprehensive planning tradition was bankrupt. Early in that decade urban poverty mounted, the cities continued to deteriorate, and the civic coalitions of the 1950s began to splinter. As the core cities of metropolitan areas grew increasingly poor and black and the suburbs increasingly middle class and white, the optimistic talk about a mid-century urban renaissance gave way to pessimistic reflections about the contemporary metropolitan crisis and to strong pressure for the development of a national urban policy.

Notes

[1] Quoted in Blake McKelvey, *The Emergence of Metropolitan America, 1915–1966* (New Brunswick, N.J.: Rutgers Univ. Press, 1968), p. 130.

[2] Quoted in Roy Lubove, *Twentieth Century Pittsburgh: Government, Business and Environmental Change* (New York: Wiley, 1969), p. 59.

[3] Quoted in Stefan Lorant, *Pittsburgh: The Story of an American City* (Garden City, N.Y.: Doubleday, 1964), p. 386.

Bibliography

Berry, Brian J. L., and Elaine Neils. "Location, Size and Shape of Cities as Influenced by Environmental Factors: The Urban Environment Writ Large," in Harvey S. Perloff, ed., *The Quality of the Urban Environment. Essays on "New Resources" in an Urban Age.* Baltimore, Md.: The Johns Hopkins Press, 1969. A precise and highly technical analysis of the American economic and urban structure after the Second World War.

Freedgood, Seymour. "New Strength in City Hall," in The Editors of Fortune, *The Exploding Metropolis.* Garden City, N.Y.: Doubleday, 1958. An argument in behalf of the "new breed" mayors.

Lowe, Jean. *Cities in a Race with Time: Progress and Poverty in America's Renewing Cities.* New York: Random House, 1967. A helpful survey of the postwar urban renaissance.

Stave, Bruce M. *The New Deal and the Last Hurrah: Pittsburgh Machine Politics.* Pittsburgh: Univ. of Pittsburgh Press, 1970. A criticism of the recent, widely accepted view that the New Deal's social and economic programs meant the beginning of the end for big-city machines and bosses.

The Contemporary 8
Metropolitan Crisis

Within a generation after the Second World War the optimistic mood that buoyed the mid-twentieth-century urban renaissance evaporated. The 1960s—"that slum of a decade," one writer called it—were punctuated not only by the emergence of a costly war in southeast Asia, a series of political and racial assassinations, and a wave of uprisings by urban blacks, but also by a revival in the sense of metropolitan crisis. Earnest students of the urban scene wrote books bearing such grim titles as *Sick Cities, The Death and Life of Great American Cities,* and *Cities in a Race with Time;* one even forecast the coming of Necropolis, the city of the dead. Toward the end of the decade the ills of the great cities had become a national obsession. In 1967 the Secretary of Agriculture devoted most of his speeches to urban problems, and in 1968

Labels in image: UPPER-INCOME FLIGHT TO SUBURBS · LOW-INCOME MIGRATION TO CITIES · TAX SQUEEZE · SHORTAGE OF RECREATION AREAS · EXODUS OF HIGH-WAGE INDUSTRIES · CRIME RISE · RISE IN JUVENILE AND AGED GROUPS · POLLUTION · TRANSPORTATION JAMS · OVERCROWDED SCHOOLS · HOUSING GHETTOS · CITIES · ©1966 HERBLOCK

"Help!"—from *The Herblock Gallery* (Simon and Schuster, 1968)

108 and 109 In a 1966 cartoon *(above)*, "cities," ringed by problems, call for help. *(facing page)* Modern Los Angeles from the air. The city embraces almost 5000 square miles.

the presidents of both the United States and the University of California, the Bishops of the United States Catholic Conference, the Republican National Convention, and *Glamour* magazine all addressed themselves at one time or another to the urban crisis.

A major factor contributing to the mounting sense of desperation was the growing recognition of the environmental implications of the postindustrial pattern of metropolitan growth. In the 1960s the most rapid urban increase continued to concentrate on the rim of the continent, and especially in the South, Southwest, and Far West. With more and more fertile, scenic, or virgin territory falling beneath the bulldozer's treads the conviction grew that such widespread urbanization would place an unbearable burden on the natural environment. Ecology now became a household word and zero population growth the rallying cry for those who feared that within a generation Americans would exhaust the continental stock of natural resources and render the North American "ecosystem" incapable of sustaining modern life. In this context the "shock city" of the 1960s was Los Angeles. Here sprawl reached such

proportions that the town was often described as a collection of suburbs in search of a city. Reformers dramatizing the dangers of smog, water shortages, traffic congestion, crime, racial discontent, or political disorganization and ineptitude invariably cited Los Angeles as the disastrous model toward which the country was drifting. And that city's mayor, Samuel Yorty, regarded early in his tenure as a potential "new breed" mayor, became by the end of the 1960s a national joke, a sure laugh for the wags of television's late-evening talk shows.

By 1970 the sense of crisis had degenerated into a general feeling of helplessness that penetrated even city hall itself. In the spring of 1969 President Richard M. Nixon summoned ten of the country's most highly regarded mayors to the White House to participate in the new administration's efforts to formulate its national urban policy. But between the time the invitations went out and the conference convened, half the mayors had indicated that they would not run again. Appalled by the crisis of confidence that gripped both urban leaders and their critics, Daniel Patrick Moynihan, the President's special advisor on urban affairs, warned that the nation seemed about to reach the self-defeating conclusion that the cities were in such bad shape that nothing could be done.

110 "Backlash" demonstrators in Chicago protest "open" public housing and the resulting influx of blacks into their neighborhood.

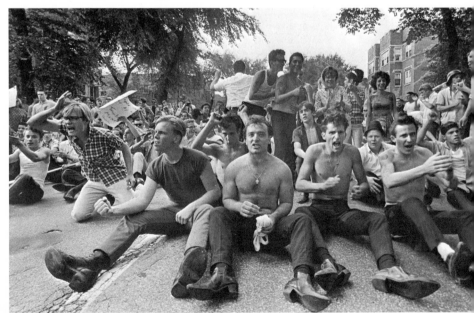

Despite the atmosphere of despair, most elements of the contemporary metropolitan crisis were neither new nor entirely unprecedented. The 1970 catalogue of urban problems read much like a reprint of the National Resources Committee report on cities in the 1930s and virtually duplicated an analysis published by Lewis Mumford in 1925. To be sure, a crisis existed in the early 1970s, but the source of its intractability rested in the contemporary configuration of a familiar aspect of the modern city, the division between the center and the periphery of the metropolis. Throughout the 1950s and 1960s and into the 1970s the suburbs attracted masses of defensive and insecure middle-class whites who embraced with new zeal the tradition of local self-government; meanwhile the core cities of metropolitan areas filled with blacks, poor whites, Chicanos, Puerto Ricans, and Indians. It was the coincidence of the city-suburban dichotomy with the question of race that frustrated efforts of political leaders to generate support for programs to overcome the basic problems of racism, unequal opportunity, and fragmented metropolitan governments that underlay other urban difficulties.

FEDERAL PROGRAMS IN THE 1960s

Paradoxically, cities reached this critical stage during a period in which the federal government devoted more attention and dollars to urban problems than ever. In 1960 John F. Kennedy ran for president on a Democratic platform that pledged federal aid for schools, medical care, depressed areas, urban transportation, housing, planning, and urban renewal. After his election both he and his successor, Lyndon B. Johnson, sought to fulfill those promises. Older programs for urban renewal, housing, water pollution control, and mass rapid transit received additional funds, the number of grants-in-aid for specific projects mushroomed, a new cabinet-level Department of Housing and Urban Development (HUD) swung into action, and President Kennedy issued a long-awaited executive order banning discrimination in all federally assisted housing projects. After Kennedy's assassination and the overwhelming Democratic victory in 1964, Congress ground out urban-oriented programs unequalled in their volume and variety. This sudden federal assault on urban problems raised expectations that the urban crisis might yet be resolved, but some of the most promising programs died before their impact could be felt, others bogged down in the tangle of overlapping intrametropolitan governments, and a few failed because they rested on a faulty analysis of the nature and direction of urban growth in postindustrial society. Meanwhile, the city-suburban split broadened, and the tensions growing out of that division deepened the sense of hopelessness, eroded the national commitment to social justice, and weakened the ability of both national parties to act decisively on urban problems.

The feverish federal activity between 1960 and 1968 in behalf of the cities amounted to more than merely devising one federal program after another in response to the urban crisis of that decade. Taken together, federal urban legislation in the Kennedy-Johnson years fell into three parts, each of which echoed earlier approaches to the resolution of urban problems. One reactivated the neighborhood preservation and participation aspect of the early-twentieth-century local-planning tradition and consisted of an attack on the poverty, discrimination, and sense of powerlessness that racked the central-city slums. The second drew on the premises of the comprehensive metropolitan planners and sought to mitigate the confusion and inefficiency of metropolitan fragmentation and to bridge the gap between city and suburban governments. The third approached the urban crisis obliquely by reviving some of the regional-planning notions of the 1920s and 1930s. It tried to alleviate crowding and poverty in the big cities and to reverse the rural-to-urban flow by spurring economic development and urban growth in the depressed sections of the countryside and by making farm and small-town life more attractive.

Renewal: Neighborhood Participation

The assault on the slums garnered the most attention. The community-centered character of the antipoverty programs had diverse origins, but one prime source lay in the mounting criticism of the urban-renewal process in the 1950s. Residents of renewal neighborhoods and their supporters became increasingly indignant about what they regarded as the haphazard and undemocratic way in which planning experts, politicians, and other "outsiders" destroyed communities, dis-

111 A neighborhood center in a New York City slum district, one manifestation of federal aid to cities in the sixties and seventies.

located people, and replaced old and deteriorated housing with huge, cold, and frequently dangerous high-rise apartment complexes in the central city. The dual mistake of merely dispersing the poor into adjacent deteriorating neighborhoods or of reconcentrating them in prison-like buildings amidst the problems of the inner city neither renewed the slums nor terminated the concentration of poverty in the cities. Both errors, opponents of the "old" urban renewal contended, could have been averted if residents of the renewal communities had been consulted and heeded in the planning process.

In 1961 and 1962 the President's Committee on Juvenile Delinquency added velocity to the growing neighborhood participation movement. Operating on the assumption that many of the problems of urban youth stemmed from an inability to develop a sense of self-confidence and dignity by making decisions that affected their lives, the Committee sponsored a number of projects in several cities, most notably Haryou in the Harlem district of New York, to test the participation hypothesis. The idea caught on, and President Johnson and his advisors laced their "War on Poverty" proposals with community projects, including the

112 Students from the City College of New York advocate community control, a major feature of which was control by residents of neighborhood school boards.

Volunteers in Service to America (VISTA), Neighborhood Youth Corps, Job Corps, local community-action commissions, and the Head Start program for preschool youngsters. All of these programs were designed to foster the "maximum feasible participation" of the poor, for the legislation and administrative guidelines stipulated that residents of target areas should be involved at all levels in planning, that neighborhood organization should be encouraged as a means of giving the poor an influential voice in all matters pertaining to their interests, and that community residents should be hired wherever possible in the various antipoverty enterprises.

The neighborhood participation experiment was crippled before it could demonstrate its effectiveness. Though popular in the central cities, maximum feasible participation of the poor aroused the opposition of a broad range of "outsiders." Professional planners and members of park, health, welfare, and other boards and agencies resented

206

the intrusion of nonexperts in the planning process. Leaders of old neighborhood associations contested bitterly for control of their constituents with the burgeoning new community groups. Politicians viewed the new organizations as threats to the power of traditional party organizations, and city officials objected both to their loss of control over federal funds and to the long meetings and painfully slow progress that maximum feasible participation entailed. A few academic critics, moreover, questioned the wisdom of placing such heavy emphasis on community organization in particular neighborhoods when some studies indicated that neighborhoods played a less significant role in the lives of slum dwellers in the postindustrial metropolis than they had earlier; others wondered if the long-range social and psychological stimulation of participation actually merited the resources that might otherwise have gone for hard material benefits. Attacked from a variety of angles and for a variety of reasons, the programs waned. In 1970 the Nixon administration, which lacked a base of voter support in the slums, seemed bent on dismantling the entire federal participation apparatus.

Countering Fragmentation

The federal attempt to reduce metropolitan political fragmentation began with the Housing and Urban Development Act of 1965. That measure provided support for area-wide planning, and the following year Congress gave HUD the power to require review of all applications for federal funds from governmental units within a given metropolitan area by a locally appointed and financed regional council or planning board. Mayor John Lindsay hastily reactivated New York's Metropolitan Regional Council, and scores of other places either followed suit or established new metropolitan transportation, health, and other agencies, some of which included representatives of city, county, and suburban governments from as many as three states. These institutions proved so cumbersome and slow-moving, however, that in 1972 no general assessment of their impact seemed possible.

Decentralization

The third part of the Democratic urban program for the 1960s took shape in 1965 with the enactment of two regional policy measures. One,

113 "Overpass," a 1966 comment on the massive allocation of federal funds to highway construction.

Overpass—from *The Herblock Gallery* (Simon and Schuster, 1968)

the Appalachian Redevelopment Act, allotted funds to highway construction on the assumption that industry and people could be attracted to chronically depressed and sparsely settled rural regions if only these places were opened up. The other set up the Economic Development Administration (EDA), which also followed a "worst-first" or place-before-people policy by focusing its aid on depressed and lightly populated regions. But the EDA also channeled funds into small "growth centers" in the hope that furthering city development would heighten economic activity in the surrounding countryside. The average population of the eighty designated growth centers in 1968 was 38,192; the median population was 24,145; and only thirteen contained more than 50,000 souls.

After the presidential election in the fall of 1968 the new Republican administration and many of its supporters enthusiastically endorsed the regional approach. President Nixon applauded the wisdom of "helping cities which have been overpopulated with migration by making the rural areas more attractive," one GOP governor talked about beginning a "rural renaissance," and a Republican senator and twenty of his colleagues introduced a series of bills to improve the general quality of American life by stimulating the development of small communities and rural areas. Yet this regional policy, too, encountered serious opposition, and the program's achievements scarcely warranted the glowing rhetoric they attracted.

Critics of the small-town development and highway construction program regarded them as unrealistic, for this approach ran counter to the process of urbanization and development in the United States. Historically, cities rather than transportation lay at the root of economic growth, and in the modern era only places containing at least 50,000 or more inhabitants exercised an influence significant enough to bring economic growth to their immediate hinterlands, while only those of 250,000 or more could sustain the job-creation function that gave them the resilience to remain viable parts of the national urban system and the human, cultural, and leisure resources to make them exciting places in which to live. Critics of this persuasion contended that the federal government never had helped and never could help the nation's big cities by urging people to leave them for much smaller and even less

114 Major regional growth centers (shown in black) by the year 2000, as envisioned by a President's Commission.

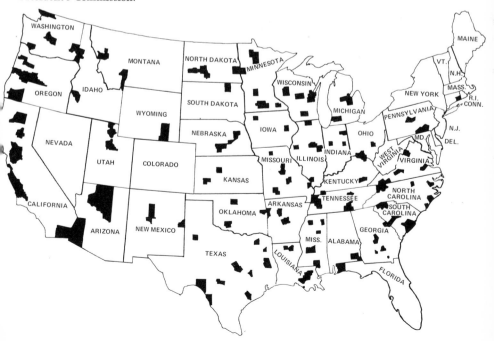

viable places. In their view a valid decentralist population policy should concentrate on assisting places of 50,000 or more inhabitants to reach the population threshold that produced self-sustaining economic diversity, the ability to lure disgruntled exiles from huge metropolises, and the power to transform their hinterlands. At the same time, these critics argued, the federal government would have to confront the problems of the inner city in these and larger places rather than leaving the slums to flounder in benign neglect while encouraging the revitalization of central business districts.

FAILURE OF FEDERAL PROGRAMS

Despite the variety and scope of the Kennedy-Johnson attack on the metropolitan crisis the programs failed to generate enough successes to develop support or to stay the deterioration of the cities. They failed, in the final analysis, because of the persisting influence of federal programs enacted in the 1950s and of policies adopted by metropolitan leadership during the postwar civic renaissance. Throughout the 1950s and early 1960s most national legislation to aid the cities helped to promote the physical expansion of the country's urban centers and to disperse the white population throughout broad suburban areas, and the Kennedy-Johnson administration was unable or unwilling to eliminate these programs, including the massive federal subsidy for superhighway construction in and around metropolitan areas. At the same time, cities across the country, like Pittsburgh, continued to adopt programs designed to revitalize downtown and to build transportation networks facilitating the movement of the white population and economic activities toward the edge of the metropolises. This federal and local commitment to centrifugal growth unaccompanied by effective measures to bring the poor into the mainstream of the economy merely exaggerated tendencies deriving from the nature of society in the postindustrial era. The net result was metropolitan sprawl, a sharpening of the racial division, and animosity between the cities and their suburbs.

CITY-SUBURB CONFLICT

By the late 1960s the persistence of the city-suburban conflict had conditioned both local and national political leaders to ignore rather than to try to resolve the critical questions of race and metropolitan fragmentation. Although the center-periphery dichotomy had first appeared during the nineteenth century, that crisis had proved manageable because the continued extension of municipal boundaries roughly kept up with the outward flow of settlement and provided the cities with the human and financial resources to mitigate the most critical problems. Under these circumstances the cities at least seemed to have a chance, but, during the 1920s, annexations declined and population growth beyond the corporate limits of the great cities exceeded that occuring within the old municipal boundaries. The Depression of the 1930s and wartime shortages temporarily stalled that process, but after the Second World War the outward surge resumed, and by 1970 over half the residents of the country's metropolises lived in suburbs. By that time, too, most students of urban life had concluded that the suburbs were in serious trouble, and these internal difficulties led suburbanites to overlook the interdependence of "urban" and "suburban" problems in the mid-twentieth century.

Simply put, the press of population into outlying districts transformed many urban problems into suburban problems. In the mid-1950s it became apparent that the inner band of more populous suburbs needed more schools, additional sewage and waste disposal facilities, and more water. In some places suburbanites were startled to discover that certain sections of the central city had more open space than they, and everywhere suburban crime rates rose, pollution spread across political boundaries, and harried automobile commuters complained that the expressways became so jammed during rush hours that they resembled gigantic parking lots. By 1970, in addition, 20 to 40 percent of the poor in many metropolises lived in suburbs, and the federal civil-rights legislation of the 1960s raised the fear that soon many blacks would be moving in, too.

Well before that threat materialized, however, beleaguered suburban officials discovered that they lacked the resources to meet the mounting problems of lagging services, congestion, and environmental pollution. Many places sought to increase their tax bases, first by admitting high-rise apartments to attract elderly, affluent, and childless residents, and then by opening the gates to "clean" industries. Yet these measures seldom sufficed, and since most suburban officials feared that annexation

211

JEFFERSO

115 A surburban billboard reflects one aspect of the "battle of the suburbs." In the language of that struggle "let's keep it that way" meant "let's keep blacks out."

or federated metropolitan government would drain their already strained tax revenues into the central cities, they turned, as they had during the Depression of the 1930s, to the federal government for grants-in-aid on special projects. But that approach proved too slow, cumbersome, and piecemeal to stay the forces of deterioration, and local officials disliked the red tape and the "strings" with which Washington bureaucrats often encumbered federal money.

Toward the end of the decade, moreover, frustration and fear in suburbia were being fed by a direct assault on the value system of the majority of the suburban population. Sociologists and novelists in the 1950s had criticized the life style and attitudes of the suburbanites as boringly bourgeois and complacent, but this time the attack came from within. By the late 1960s a significant proportion of the young and the women of the suburbs were in revolt against suburban culture and loyalties. The suburbs contributed a disproportionately large share of the membership to both the Students for a Democratic Society and the women's liberation movement, and while some self-styled urban sophisticates still defined the suburbs as the region of broad lawns and narrow minds, many suburban youths raised hard questions about the morality of the Vietnam war, the politics of compromise, and the persistence of poverty and inequality in central cities ringed by affluence.

s the good life
t's keep it
at way

NELON
ONVICH
LLERE
ENDENT TEAM

Yet few suburbanites of any age or sex seemed willing to attack these basic social, economic, racial, and ethical questions through the political and governmental system. A nationwide poll finding that the proportion of the public with a high level of trust in government dropped from 64 percent in 1964 to 35 percent in 1970 indicated that most people had lost faith in major national leaders and parties. Instead of registering their grievances through traditional political or governmental channels, increasing numbers of citizens joined the swelling revolt against the "Establishment."

After 1964 the spirit of participatory democracy and citizen activism spread from the central-city ghettos across the face of the metropolis as a wide variety of groups organized to make their voices heard on matters that they felt most affected their lives. The strong sense of black pride crystallized a new ethnic consciousness among second-, third-, and fourth-generation immigrants who occupied outer city wards or lower-middle-income suburbs not far from the bulging ghettos. Other interest groups from similar residential districts took to the streets and filled meeting halls to protest sex education in the schools, pornography, and disrespect for the flag or the policeman's badge. Activist youngsters from more affluent enclaves tried to make the nature of American culture a major issue. They distrusted traditional hierarchical authority,

213

favored personal and social experimentation, and demanded a voice in basic educational decisions and the right of 18-year-olds to vote.

Political Instability

Though the broad quest for control that the suburban citizens' participation movement of the late 1960s represented took most contemporaries by surprise, basic distrust of the "system" began a decade before. It first manifested itself, however, in the weakening of party ties. Increasingly, on election day the voters punished the party in power for not responding to their anxieties, and in the process eroded the ability of either of the two parties to function as a cohesive force through which basic questions that lay at the root of the electorate's discontent could be raised, debated, and acted upon. Confronted with a fickle and factionalized electorate, political leadership splintered and the two-party system drifted toward paralysis.

The undermining of the traditional American political system began in the 1950s when the flight to suburbia first reached proportions significant enough to influence national elections. Initially the Republicans, the national minority party since 1932, benefited from the suburban movement. In national politics the suburbs had always supported Republican candidates, and there seemed every reason to believe that they would continue to do so in the postwar era. Many of the new suburbanites were former residents of rock-ribbed Republican rural areas or small towns, and most of the rest were ex-big-city Democrats who, according to the prevailing "conversion theory," would become steadfast supporters of the GOP once they moved into the middle-class respectability and Republican atmosphere of the suburban districts. Presidential election returns during the 1950s seemed to confirm this prognosis. The Eisenhower victories of 1952 and 1956 comprised, in fact, the initial expression in national politics of the new suburban power. Ike's support there, combined with the residual vote of the farms and small towns, enabled the Republicans to overcome the coalition of the poor, ethnics, blacks, and workers of the cities with the solid South, which had formed the foundation for the Democratic hold on the White House from 1932 through 1948. The suburban explosion, it seemed, had given the Republicans a secure national majority.

Developments in the next decade shattered both the conversion theory and the notion that suburbia was homogeneous, politically stable, affluent, and trouble-free. In 1960, John Kennedy, a Democrat, won the presidency in an extremely tight race because he was able to contrive small majorities in some suburbs and reduce the Republican margin in others, and Johnson's landslide victory in 1964 rested on solid suburban support. There were several reasons for the Democrats' better showing in the suburbs, including discontent stemming from the rising population density in peripheral districts. Beyond that, however, most lower-middle-income Democrats leaving big cities settled in new suburban developments among people like themselves. Having changed neither their economic status nor their neighbors, they felt no compulsion to alter their politics. And many upwardly mobile Democrats moving into the older middle- to upper-middle-income and Wasp suburbs also stayed with the Democratic Party. More often than not these newcomers bore ethnic names and belonged to a non-Protestant religion, and the Republican majority gave them a cool reception. The newly arrived head of the house found it difficult to borrow a rake or a lawnmower, his wife had even less luck in cracking the ladies' bridge clubs, and his children discovered that they were second-rate citizens when it came to participating in the routine of extracurricular activities in the suburban schools. Expecting a warm handshake, the former Democrats from the big city were greeted instead with a medium "hello." Thus in different ways many of the new residents in both the development and the establishment suburbs had their Democratic predispositions reinforced rather than reduced by their experience in a novel environment.

Though the new Democratic strength in the suburbs convinced many that the party had successfully bridged the gap between the cities and the suburbs, the regular Democratic organization soon discovered it could not assume that former big-city Democrats would provide the kind of strict party loyalty they had enjoyed in the old days. Eugene McCarthy's 1968 "children's crusade" against Johnson, the war in Vietnam, and the "old" politics gathered its principal strength from suburbs like those around Gary, Indianapolis, Los Angeles, and San Francisco, and Richard Nixon owed his narrow victory that fall to defections among "Democratic" suburban voters.

Startled by the sudden dissolution of the Democratic metropolitan majority, political scientists looked back over long-range election trends and discovered that after 1948 party fealty no longer satisfied the political needs of a broad range of middle Americans as it had in the age of FDR. In the five presidential elections between 1932 and 1948 almost 51 percent of the counties in the nation, including nearly all those in major metropolitan areas, cast a majority of their votes for the same party's candidate each time. But in the five elections from 1952 through 1968 only one-fifth of the counties stayed with the same party's nominee, and all five of these contests were either extremely close or landslides. In the same time span, moreover, the proportion of voters who listed themselves as "independent" rose from 22 percent to 31 percent, and those voters came predominantly from the better-educated and more prosperous segments of the population. These election and registration figures indicated that the electorate of the outer wards and suburban districts had increasingly abandoned party regularity in the 1950s and 1960s in favor of using both parties to protect their interests.

By becoming first "free-floating" voters and, in the late 1960s, participating activists, a broad range of Americans exerted pressure on their private version of the Establishment to respect their varied desires and anxieties. In so doing they responded to a deep-seated craving to control what they perceived as chaos, to make the future both manageable and beneficent. But they also weakened the two-party system without devising an effective alternative. At the end of the 1960s the gap between the city and the suburbs remained appallingly wide, and the spirit of divisiveness and political instability within the suburbs blocked the creation of effective metropolitan and federal programs.

Revenue Sharing: For and Against

Political instability and discontent in the suburbs and a shortage of resources with which to handle their problems forced political strategists to seek out policies that might assist and unite the peripheral districts. Many thought a "local-control" program stood the best chance, and the Supreme Court's one-man, one-vote decision in the early 1960s mandating reapportionment of state legislative and congressional districts seemed to provide a way to make that feasible. Since rearrangement of political boundaries in the wake of the Court's decision strengthened the suburban voice in the state capitols and in Congress at the expense of the big cities, it was no coincidence that the talk about a "new federalism," which had surfaced in the 1950s, now began to center on "revenue sharing," a scheme by which federal funds could be channeled back into the hands of state and local government officials. After reapportionment, revenue sharing acquired a special charm for suburbanites. If adopted, they felt, it would enable the thousands of governments in the outer metropolitan ring to exercise their new political strength to secure the lion's share of the federal money. The major potential losers, on the other hand, were the big cities.

The controversy over revenue sharing brought the city-suburban division into clear focus. Critics of the scheme attacked it on several counts. Some, noting that suburban governments operated without benefit of the day-by-day scrutiny given big-city officials by powerful, well-staffed metropolitan daily newspapers and various good-government associations in the central cities, contended that revenue sharing would usher in an age of suburban corruption rivaling that in the big cities of the late nineteenth century. Others argued that the nonpartisan style of politics that predominated in the suburbs had failed to produce a political system capable of making decisions on the location of streetlights let alone on the more complex issues of housing, pollution, and poverty. Still others raised the old concern about the fragmented metropolitan governmental structure. The metropolis, they argued, was a single, interdependent entity, and any rational system of government ought to recognize that social and economic reality and be organized in such a way that the revenue produced by the region would be spent so that it met the pressing needs of the whole district, not the particular needs of some of its parts.

The most telling criticism of revenue sharing hit at the most dangerous dimension of the division between the city and suburbs. Raised by those who believed that the question of race and the ghetto comprised the basic domestic issues facing metropolitan America in the 1970s, it rejected the revenue-sharing formula for tax redistribution because of its potential for producing an essentially static metropolis. These critics pointed out that the suburban population was overwhelmingly

white and that the central cities were fast becoming the private pre-
serves of blacks and of nonwhite persons generally. In their view, any
program that might allocate most federal resources to the generally
prosperous and overwhelmingly white suburbs would perpetuate the
city-suburban dichotomy, encourage the growth of the ghettos, intensify
metropolitan racial tensions, polarize the country, and sow the seeds
for a generation of violent domestic discord. In this perspective any
metropolitan reform that did not contribute to the elimination of in-
voluntary residential segregation by race would be futile.

Background: Black Residential Patterns

The Nineteenth Century   The case against perpetuating the ghetto
rested upon the long, peculiar, and bitter history of American urban
blacks. Jim Crow became the rule in American cities before the Civil
War. Though specific patterns varied from city to city, in the mid-nineteenth century places of public accommodation were segregated in
North and South alike. Residential distribution reflected this tendency
to push blacks to the margins of town life. Even in the South, where urban slaveholders dispersed slave dwellings across the city as a means of
preventing social organization and united movements among blacks,
the blacks seeking release from constant surveillance escaped the master's eye by accumulating in enclaves on the edge of the cities. The same
pattern developed in northern urban centers, and in both sections
these scattered and diminutive ghettos formed vulnerable targets for the
attacks of Negrophobic mobs of native lower-class whites and immigrants who competed daily with blacks for jobs and housing within the
crowded boundaries of the walking city.

Not surprisingly, the proportion of blacks in the total population of
most southern and many northern cities was declining as the last half
of the nineteenth century began. In this perspective, perhaps the most
dramatic event of the post–Civil War years was the reversal of the
"bleaching-out" process and the beginning of the long migration of
southern rural blacks into the cities. There they established families,
organized a variety of social institutions, sought jobs and education,
and pressed their demands for acceptance into the mainstream.

They faced formidable obstacles. The white response, generated by
fear of the black influx and a tenacious set of attitudes developed be-

fore the war, was overwhelmingly and everywhere hostile. A strong segment of white opinion still insisted on the exclusion of blacks from access to public life and the educational and welfare facilities of the cities. Pressured by the fact or threat of federal intervention during the civil-rights drive of the Reconstruction period, that position gradually softened. But the authorities in Washington also backed away from equal justice before the law and settled for an unwritten federal-urban racial compromise. By its terms the races would share the cities, but on a separate and scarcely equal basis.

Blacks, though they had the vote and made up from 25 to 50 percent of the total population in some southern cities before 1880, found it impossible to alter the terms of the compromise. Residential patterns help explain their weakness. They still inhabited, for the most part, miniature ghettos among the peripheral slums and remained subject to mob action and small-scale but daily harassment by whites in adjacent neighborhoods. Black leaders, moreover, found it difficult to unite the scattered population and meager resources of the black neighborhoods for a concentrated program of economic, educational, religious, or political self-help. Divided, the blacks seemed helpless and their future bleak as the nineteenth century drew to a close.

116   A residential street in Harlem—one of New York's black ghettos—about 1920. Many of these buildings are still occupied.

Yet the situation was not static. As the modern city took shape during the last quarter of the century, whites pushed out toward the new urban fringe and blacks were left behind in the old and decaying sections of the central city. In addition, the heightened pace of the black rural-to-urban migration expanded the old black enclaves and brought about their merger. By 1900, urban blacks of all classes found their lives increasingly circumscribed by the boundaries of the inner-city ghetto.

The Twentieth Century   The reversal of the familiar geographic arrangement of the urban population in the emerging modern city produced significant and far-reaching changes for both whites and blacks. First, a small but influential minority of prosperous white business and professional men and women in southern cities began to advocate a more just implementation of the separate-but-equal doctrine. Comfortably separated physically from the dark ghettos, these reformers from the periphery manned the new interracial civic committees, proposed an enlarged and improved system of public and private social work among blacks, supported the establishment of secondary educational facilities for blacks, denounced lynching, and fought the municipal residential segregation ordinances designed to prevent blacks from moving into the better spots available in contiguous districts and in outlying suburban regions. In northern cities similar groups of white reformers went beyond that program and pressed for equal rights and encouraged black economic, social, and cultural achievement and advancement as well.

They faced stiff odds. The middle- and lower-class whites who lived close to the cutting edge of the burgeoning black districts refused to go along. Residential vulnerability, as much as any other single factor, explains their reluctance, and their numbers made them a potent political force. For many, their recently acquired and hard-earned residential status beyond the slums functioned as a surrogate for the economic and social advances that still lay beyond their reach. Caught between slum and suburb, the whites of the Zone of Emergence proved ready prey for the race demagogue in politics and in the twentieth-century Klan. And as blacks approached their "turf" they burned crosses, bombed houses purchased by blacks in transitional neighborhoods, pressured realtors to uphold the color line, and either pushed for residential seg-

117 Black leader W. E. B. DuBois stands *(at right)* in the office of his magazine *Crisis* about 1910. The magazine, which achieved a circulation of 100,000, was active in the cause of civil rights for blacks.

regation laws or added racial covenants to home mortgages and deeds. Not infrequently they broke loose in savage race riots like those during the "red summer" of 1919.

During the same span of years the emergence of the inner-city ghetto set the stage for the development of a new, more powerful, and more aggressive drive for freedom led by those successful blacks who had done everything society expected of them but had been denied the benefits. The growing black urban population, the enlarged physical scale of the inner-city ghettos, the development of virulent Negrophobia in the Zone of Emergence, and the appearance of a handful of white allies on the periphery of the city indicated to a new generation of black leaders that something had to and could be done to improve the conditions under which they and their people lived. Disfranchised in the South and everywhere denied the right and opportunity to move up in the urban social structure and beyond the reach of the slums, the "talented tenth" turned back into the ghetto to organize a push to improve the quality of life and prevent all blacks, regardless of their educational or economic achievements, from being permanently relegated to second-class citizenship.

221

Though strategies and goals varied, between 1890 and 1930 the black bourgeoisie in cities across the country organized an imposing array of clubs, societies, and associations. Whatever their programs or the economic and occupational levels of their members, these groups stressed above all race pride, racial unity, and achievement. The urban groundwork had been laid for a series of national alliances institutionalized by 1920 in such diverse organizations as the National Association for the Advancement of Colored People, the National Urban League, the National Negro Business League, the National Federation of Colored Women's Clubs, the Association for the Study of Negro Life and History, and Marcus Garvey's black nationalist movement, the Universal Negro Improvement Association.

Although optimism about the potential of the "new Negro" movement ran high, a retrospective assessment of its successes turns up little of real significance. In 1930 antiblack discrimination continued in its traditional forms and the ghettos remained intact. The Great Depression made matters even worse. Nonetheless, two generations of activism had raised black aspirations and provided valuable schooling in urban leadership. And in the years following the Depression it seemed that some of the hopes might at last be fulfilled.

High levels of employment during the Second World War, the gradual broadening of opportunities in the armed forces, and the general affluence of the 1950s produced a small but important increase in the number of urban blacks achieving middle-class status. A trickle of desegregation and antidiscrimination decisions by the courts over the same span of years wedged the door of opportunity open a bit farther. Yet the Second World War and the 1950s also brought another great flood of rural black migrants into the cities. White resistance to residential desegregation stiffened, and the black ghettos swelled and deteriorated. And as the urban-renewal programs of the 1950s took hold, thousands of blacks were rooted out of the slums with virtually no provision for relocation in other neighborhoods. They pushed, instead, into old and dilapidated districts recently abandoned by the outwardly mobile whites.

Thus, in the 1950s the blacks were victims of a bitter paradox. As their expectations and aspirations rose, the big-city ghettos expanded.

Smoldering with frustration and bitterness, the inner-city ghettos exploded in violence during the 1960s. In 1965 the Watts riot shook Los Angeles and the nation. And in that summer and for five summers thereafter portions of the black districts of Newark, Detroit, Rochester, New York, Cincinnati, Washington, and a hundred other places went up in flames. This time, however, whites did not carry the violence. Instead, angry blacks struck out at the symbols of white oppression that dotted the ghetto districts, including police, firemen, white-owned businesses, and government agencies.

The white response varied. City police departments expanded both their riot training and their community relations programs. The federal government under Kennedy and Johnson pushed hard to enact and enforce civil-rights legislation and to provide jobs and educational opportunities for inner-city blacks. On the metropolitan periphery, well removed from the turmoil and violence close to downtown, nervous

118 In 1965 whole blocks of buildings burn during the rioting in Watts, a black district of Los Angeles.

119   One of 20,000 children who live in Chicago's Taylor Homes surveys some of the 31
identical high-rise buildings that compose the slum-clearance housing project.

white homeowners purchased weapons and many joined the "backlash" and "law and order" campaigns advocated by local and national
political figures.

By 1970 it was difficult to predict what might come next. But the
underlying cause of the riots was clear. A 1967 presidential commission
on civil disorders, the so-called Kerner Commission on the ghetto riots
of the 1960s, concluded that white racism, in the final analysis, was
responsible for the uprisings. The Commission was on the mark. Like
other Americans, natives and immigrants alike, blacks had, since the
mid-nineteenth century, become an increasingly urban people. But unlike other Americans, they knew that even if they somehow managed
to secure an education, acquire a decent job, and build a cohesive family, neither they nor their children were likely to escape the confines
of the ghetto. After six generations of experience in American cities
even the most successful blacks were still restricted to the worst neigh-

borhoods. They knew that for them the ghetto was not to be a staging ground for mobility. In the twentieth century the realization of that fact produced a strong drive to get into the "mainstream," some violence, and a swelling chorus of cries for revolution and black nationalism. In 1970 it was not entirely clear which of these directions "the movement" would take next, and an outbreak of rioting among Mexican-Americans in Los Angeles during the winter of 1971 suggested that white racism might be affecting Chicanos and other nonwhite metropolitan minorities in much the same way it had the blacks. But the black experience in metropolitan America supports the view, as Professor Richard C. Wade put it, that

> the growth of the ghetto is the central domestic problem of American life. Not only does it stand mockingly as a symbol of the unfulfilled promise of equality, but it also frustrates the attack on other metropolitan issues. For decisions on such questions as education, housing, and poverty are caught up in the controversy over civil rights and are often deflected or postponed.[1]

THE 1970s: CONTINUING CRISIS

As the 1970s opened, the country floundered in the midst of still another urban crisis. Yet the history of the modern city in America since 1840 offered some encouragement. The problems of the cities in the early 1970s were not entirely new, and many were not as severe in the mid-twentieth century as they had been in the mid-nineteenth. A few respected urban specialists even claimed that the contemporary metropolis was cleaner, safer, more pleasant, and less congested than its predecessor by 50 or 100 years. The time, however, in which to resolve the question of race and other metropolitan issues had grown perilously short. With each day, as the line between the city and suburb increasingly conformed to the division between black and white, the sense of metropolitan crisis deepened, the threat to the survival of the ideals of democracy and equality in America grew more acute, and the hard and complex question of working out a national urban policy for the last quarter of the twentieth century became more difficult.

In the last half of the twentieth century, as in the last half of the nineteenth, the heart of the urban crisis lay in the division between the center and the periphery of the metropolis. But the structural setting and psychological context of the post-1945 crisis differed sharply from the old. At the turn of the century the most critical inner-city minorities problem involved white foreign-born residents, not "indelible immigrants" barred irrevocably from their right to move freely into metropolitan life by the color of their skins. Turn-of-the-century cities offered newcomers a multiplicity of jobs requiring little or no skill or formal education, and those jobs could be found in central as well as in peripheral districts. But in the postindustrial era only those well equipped with technological, managerial, or communications skills could take advantage of the positions that replaced the declining number of simpler tasks, and the businesses providing those opportunities continued to retreat to sites on the rims of urban settlements. In the early 1900s the option of annexation remained open for cities struggling to finance needed services, and the embryo planning profession generated schemes for neighborhood reconstruction and comprehensive and regional planning that commanded widespread and enthusiastic support. Three generations later the mania for local self-government in the suburbs blocked annexation and perpetuated deep social, economic, cultural, and racial cleavages within metropolises. Those divisions, in turn, heightened and spread a sense of insecurity and spawned separationist ideologies that turned the neighborhood participation and citizen activist movements toward defensive and narrowly defined programs whose advocates slighted the fundamental fact of metropolitan interdependence. Planners, meanwhile, like public officials generally, lost their confidence, credibility, and sense of direction as a wide range of dissatisfied elements in the cities and the suburbs leveled a steady fire of criticism at the "social engineers" and bureaucrats for failing to alleviate the familiar litany of urban problems.

The new discontents of the late 1960s and early 1970s added more complex dimensions to the festering dissatisfaction of the post-1945 period. By the late 1960s the turn-of-the-century nostalgia for country life and the rural frontier gave way to a new nostalgia—one that longed for cities that never existed, cities of stable, serene, safe neighborhoods built more to the human scale. But the new nostalgia fed on a broader surge of fear than the old and sapped the confidence of the country in

120 An 1899 prediction of how New York City would look 100 years later. The artist showed a remarkable prescience but a retarded time sense: the congestion shown was reached in only half the time.

its ability to overcome the urban crisis. That fear and timidity stemmed from several sources: The anomaly of spiraling inflation in a period of high unemployment contributed to the growing national mood of frustration; dissatisfactions about unequally distributed tax burdens increased; and anxieties about the ecological crisis, overpopulation, and the opening of the age of zero economic growth fostered a Malthusian paranoia about the ability of the nation to provide for all its citizens and revitalize the American dream.

Clearly, solutions to pressing metropolitan problems, like the resolution of the crisis of confidence, lay beyond the means of neighborhoods, cities, suburbs, or even metropolitan regions or states. Each of these   227 units might do its part, but the mid-twentieth-century metropolitan crisis required a national urban policy. Yet the twentieth-century metropolitan reform tradition provided little substantive guidance for developing a policy, and in 1970 neither major political party seemed capable of rallying a solid majority coalition around a program for innovative, decisive, enlightened, humane, just, and constructive action. In this perspective the metropolitan prospect seemed grim indeed. During the mid-nineteenth century, in the midst of another urban crisis, a similar paralysis of the national political system produced a Civil War, which pitted section against section, and the more pessimistic commentators in the mid-twentieth century feared that the crisis of the 1970s might culminate in an open conflict between city and suburb. Whether conflict would be contained, postponed, or ultimately dispelled remained to be seen. But in 1972 it seemed evident that neither maintaining the status quo nor launching a quest to fulfill a fundamentally antimetropolitan nostalgia for the little community and local autonomy constituted an adequate response to the challenge.

Notes

[1] Richard C. Wade, "Urbanization," in C. Vann Woodward, ed., *The Comparative Approach to American History* (New York: Basic Books, 1968), p. 202.

Bibliography

Bracey, John H., Jr., August Meier, and Elliott Rudwick, eds. *The Rise of the Ghetto.* Belmont, Calif.: Wadsworth, 1971. Traces the growth of black ghettos from the early nineteenth century through the 1960s.

The Editors of Fortune. *The Exploding Metropolis: A Study of the Assault on Urbanism and How Our Cities Can Resist It.* Garden City, N.Y.: Doubleday, 1958. An expression of the crisis of confidence in the resiliency of cities shadowed by expressions of the "new nostalgia."

Fogelson, Robert M. *Violence as Protest: A Study of Riots and Ghettoes.* Garden City, N.Y.: Doubleday, 1971. An interpretation of racial violence in the 1960s. Contains analyses of who rioted, why, and the dilemma of black moderates and white liberals.

Gordon, Mitchell. *Sick Cities: Psychology and Pathology of American Urban Life.* Baltimore, Md.: Penguin Books, 1966. A depressing journalistic statement of the plight of the cities in the 1960s.

Jacobs, Jane. *The Death and Life of Great American Cities.* New York: Random House, 1961. A stinging attack on American planners that is motivated in large part by the "new nostalgia." Stimulating and on the mark much of the time.

Moynihan, Daniel Patrick, ed. *Toward a National Urban Policy.* New York: Basic Books, 1970. Contains two important and subtle analyses of the current metropolitan crisis by Mr. Moynihan. The other essays, all contributed by distinguished urban specialists, provide thoughtful analyses of specific aspects of the crisis.

Wood, Robert C. *Suburbia: Its People and Their Politics.* Boston: Houghton Mifflin, 1958. A critical yet not entirely unsympathetic analysis of the suburban "problem."

General Bibliography

Glaab, Charles N. "The Historian and the American City: A Bibliographic Survey," in Philip M. Hauser and Leo F. Schnore, eds., *The Study of Urbanization.* New York: Wiley, 1965. A concise survey of the varieties of urban history, and an introduction to the "state of the art" among urban specialists in other social sciences.

———— and A. Theodore Brown. *A History of Urban America.* New York: Macmillan, 1967. The only general urban history text. Readable and free of jargon.

Higham, John, Leonard Krieger, and Felix Gilbert. *History: The Development of Historical Studies in the United States.* Englewood Cliffs, N.J.: Prentice-Hall, 1965. The section by Higham constitutes a good recent account of the major directions in the writing of American history since the late nineteenth century.

Hoover, Dwight. "The Diverging Paths of American Urban History," in Raymond A. Mohl and Neil Betten, eds., *Urban America in Historical Perspective.* New York: Weybright and Talley, 1970. Links the writing of urban history to developments among urban specialists in the other social sciences and assesses the strengths and weaknesses of urban history.

Jackson, Kenneth T. and Stanley K. Schultz. *Cities in American History.* New York: Knopf, 1972. The best of several collections of essays on urban history. Many of the pieces were specially commissioned for this volume, and the interpretive thrust is compatible with that presented in *The Urbanization of America.*

Mayer, Harold M. and Richard C. Wade. *Chicago: The Growth of a Metropolis.* Chicago: The Univ. of Chicago Press, 1969. The best one-volume illustrated history of a single city. Its integration of text and illustrative materials effectively portrays the significance of the spatial dimension of urban life.

Tunnard, Christopher and Henry H. Reed, Jr. *American Skyline: The Growth and Form of Our Cities and Towns.* Boston: Houghton Mifflin, 1955. A useful brief survey of American urban history from an architectural and planning perspective.

Wade, Richard C. "An Agenda for Urban History," in George Athan Billias and Gerald N. Grob, eds., *American History: Retrospect and Prospect.* New York: The Free Press, 1971. The best single piece on the rise of urban history, its place in American historical writing, its relationship to the "pathology" approach of other urban specialists, its contributions to our understanding of American history and the tasks ahead.

————. "Urbanization," in C. Vann Woodward, ed., *The Comparative Approach to American History.* New York: Basic Books, 1968. Ranges over most of the American past, but concentrates on the emergence of the "new city" in the nineteenth century and the history of the center-periphery conflict into the long hot summers of the mid-1960s.

PHOTO CREDITS

232

Index